CW00951681

What's being said about Intelligent

"…the team at Intelligent Enterprise has built a process that has value no matter where you are along the path to Managed Services."

"Their methodology can save months and months of wandering aimlessly along the path to implementing Managed Services, and help your organization avoid a landscape full of minefields along the way."

"I recommend you closely evaluate the information they have developed and determine how it can impact your company."

Arlin Sorenson, President - Heartland Technology Solutions

"Intelligent Enterprise's Guide To Managed Services was so clear and thought out, I was able to start implementing Managed Services in two months instead of 2 years."

"Intelligent Enterprise's experience, pre-built systems and templates has saved me years of development time."

"With Intelligent Enterprise's Managed Services methodology, Adkins Technologies is the Nordstrom's of IT consulting."

Eric Adkins, President - Adkins Technologies

"To understand Managed Services is to realize the benefits of recurring IT revenue and thus a real business valuation. Intelligent Enterprise's Guide delivers on this statement."

"Intelligent Enterprise's Guide to Managed Services helps transform an IT job into an IT business."

"It's the perfect method to both expand your new or established IT business."

Dave Siebert, President - IT Innovators

The Guide To A Successful Managed Services Practice

"Packed with lots of valuable tools and other information that would have likely taken years to acquire on our own..."

"The Managed Services Guide from Intelligent Enterprise is a "must-have" for any organization considering offering proactive, flat rate IT services."

"Intelligent Enterprise's Guide To Managed Services helped us to bring great clarity to our own Managed Services offering."

Kurt Sippel, President – Applied Tech Solutions

"We found, using Intelligent Enterprise's model, it is easy to communicate the value to our customers."

"Once we met with Intelligent Enterprise we connected all of the dots..."

"In the 90 days since our first consultation with Intelligent Enterprise, we sold 4 new accounts with our "all-you-can-eat" Managed Services IT outsourcing service."

Phil Kenealy, President – ACES

"Intelligent Enterprise's Guide shows both the technical and business processes needed to succeed in a managed services business."

"Their methodology details all of the elements necessary to success in managed services, including marketing, sales, planning, implementation and follow-up."

"As a successful managed services provider, Intelligent Enterprise unlocked many of the secrets necessary to operate a profitable managed services business."

Jim W. Locke, Principal – JW Locke & Assoc

President – SMB Technology Network™

**Intelligent Enterprise's
Managed Services Series**

The Guide to a Successful Managed Services Practice

- What Every SMB IT Service Provider Should Know

Volume One

Introduction

Erick Simpson

The Guide To A Successful Managed Services Practice

MSP University

7077 Orangewood Avenue, Suite 104

Garden Grove, CA 92841

www.mspu.us

Voice: (714) 898-8195

Fax: (714) 898-8194

10 9 8 7 6 5 4 3 2

Printed in the United States of America

ISBN 0-9788943-0-8

Library of Congress Control Number: 2007942048
Library of Congress subject heading:
Computer Consulting

Contents

To receive the downloadable forms, tools and collateral discussed in this book, as well as exclusive additional sales and marketing resources and valuable webinar training absolutely FREE, register your copy of The Guide to a Successful Managed Services Practice at www.mspu.us/bookregistration today!

About the Author

As Co-founder, Vice President and CIO of Intelligent Enterprise and MSP University, Erick Simpson has experienced first-hand the challenges of growing an I.T. Business. Intelligent Enterprise has been providing Information Technology Solutions to the Southern California SMB Market since 1997. Their relationships with  partners such as Microsoft, Cisco, Citrix and HP have allowed them the ability to design, scale and implement effective infrastructure solutions for their diverse client base.

Intelligent Enterprise, a Microsoft Gold Certified and Business Solutions Partner and Small Business Specialist, successfully migrated to a Managed Services business model in January of 2005. Prior to this, they were operating as many other I.T. Providers have – reacting to Clients in "break-fix" mode, and dealing with the constant demand to recruit new clients and sell new solutions each and every month in order to meet their receivables goals.

Intelligent Enterprise developed an "All You Can Eat" Managed Services Approach focused on 3 Core Deliverables – Remote Help Desk, Proactive Network Monitoring, and they pioneered Vendor Management. Through the creation of a Managed Services Sales and Marketing approach unique to the Industry, Intelligent Enterprise sold over $2MM worth of Managed Services Agreements before being asked to share their Managed Services knowledge and expertise with hundreds of IT Service Providers, Vendors and Channel Organizations worldwide through their Managed Services University at www.mspu.us.

MSP University has helped numerous manufacturer, vendor, distributor and franchise membership organizations, their channels, and thousands of independent IT service organizations worldwide educate themselves in transitioning IT service businesses to successful, profitable managed services practices through its educational, training, fulfillment and consulting services.

A recognized author, speaker and trainer, and contributor to Microsoft's Small Business Channel Community Expert Column and presenter of a continuing series of Microsoft, Intel Cisco and Ingram Micro workshops, events and webcasts on managed services, Erick is the author of the follow-ups in MSP University's Managed Service Series; "The Best I.T. Sales & Marketing BOOK EVER!", focused on helping I.T. and managed services providers grow their businesses through effective passive and direct marketing techniques proven to win business and increase revenues, and "The Best I.T. Service Delivery BOOK EVER!, focused on improving I.T. and managed services providers' business success through building, maintaining, maximizing and migrating their service delivery models for maximum efficiency, effectiveness and profitability.

Erick's professional certifications include Microsoft MCP and SBSC, and affiliations include SMBTN and HTG1 Peer Group Memberships. Erick has conducted nationwide Managed Services workshops, boot camps and presentations at industry events such as the Microsoft Worldwide Partner Conference, SMBNation, SMBSummit, ITPro Conference, ITAlliance, ICCA, MSP Revolution and others.

Erick also co-authored Arlin Sorensen's HTG Peer Group book *"Peer Power – Powerful Ideas for Partners from Peers "*, available at www.htgmembers.com, and his recent articles on Managed Services are available at the following web urls:

- Maximize Service Delivery Profits During Economic Downturns – Author, MSPMentor July 2008 - http://www.mspmentor.net/wp-content/uploads/2008/06/maximizing-service-delivery-profits-during-economic-downturnsdoc.pdf
- We Can't Just Sell Managed Services – Author, MSPMentor June 2008 - http://www.mspmentor.net/wp-content/uploads/2008/06/we-can-t-just-sell-managed-servicesdoc.pdf
- The Importance of Vertical-Specific Marketing for MSP's – Author, Focus On MSP May 2008 - http://www.focusonmsp.com/articles/20080415-3.aspx
- Managed Services, your business plan and you – Author, SearchITChannel July 2007 - http://searchitchannel.techtarget.com/general/0,295582,sid96_gci1262243,00.html
- Managed Services – What's All the Buzz About? Author, Microsoft Small Business Channel Community - https://partner.microsoft.com/us/40029753
- Managed Services – It Makes Sense – Author, ChannelPro June 2007 – http://www.channelpro-digital.com/channelpro/200706/?folio=38
- An Introduction To Managed Services – Author, Infotech Update January 2007 – http://infotech.aicpa.org/NR/rdonlyres/AC23261D-D7F4-4459-A822-DFD4FDA8F999/0/it_jan_feb07.pdf

Erick lives in Orange County, California with his wife Susan and their two sons, Connor and Riley. His prior technical experience includes overseeing the design, development and implementation of Enterprise-level Help Desks and Call Centers for Fortune 1000 organizations.

Dedication

This book, the first in our Managed Services Series, is dedicated to all Small Business Specialists and SMB IT Service Providers grappling with the decision to transition their current business model to an Annuity-Based Managed Services model, as well as to existing Managed Services Providers seeking to increase their knowledge through the experiences and methodologies of others.

Acknowledgements

I'd like to take a moment to acknowledge the following persons who have either directly or indirectly influenced our adoption and implementation of a Managed Services training and support system for SMB IT Service Providers. These appear in no particular order:

Arlin Sorenson, Phil Kenealy, Mitch Miller, Kurt Sippel, Dave Cooksey, Don Miller, Dan Hay, Gavin Steiner, Jim Strickland, John Pritchard, Don Miller, Dan Shundoff, Jim W. Locke, Dave Siebert, Eric Adkins, John Rubino, Tim Larocque, Sean Sweeney, Carlson Colomb, Stephen Alford, Ron Grattop, Christopher Goebel, Akash Saraf, Clinton Gatewood, Rajeev Laghate, Harry Brelsford, Beatrice Mulzer, Nancy Williams, Jeff Middleton, Vlad Mazek, John Chasse, Brian Barnes, Karl Palachuk, Amy Luby, Dr. Gregory H. Wong and Robin Robins.

I'd also especially like to recognize Amir Bouzardjomehri, Enrique Sandoval, Matthew Harshbarger, Jennifer Rodgers, Tiffany Trevillison and Kristi Heicke, as well as all of our

Managed Services Partners, Fulfillment Partners and Vendors, who continue to provide us with excellent feedback and ideas, as we work to develop and improve our Managed Services Training and Support Services Offerings.

Thank you all for your continued inspiration and support.

Foreword

A considerable number of SMB IT Service Providers have built their Practices over the years based upon a Reactive Service Delivery, or "Break-Fix" business model. Based on the formula of trading time for money, this model may serve the SMB IT Service Provider's immediate income-generating needs, but it also hampers their ability to scale without requiring additional Staff or other resources. If the SMB IT Service Provider wishes to remain successful and grow their business in today's competitive IT landscape, an attractive option is to transition to an Annuity-Based, Proactive Managed IT Service delivery model.

Unfortunately, there is currently no single resource that these Service Providers can turn to, in order to guide them through this challenging transition. In addition, many have become comfortable and/or complacent with their existing reactive business model, and as a result, are likely to experience additional difficulty in transitioning to a Proactive Managed IT Service delivery model.

Our goal with this Managed Services Series is to deliver the type of meaningful information on the Managed Services model that was sorely lacking when we began searching for an alternative to our own reactive "break-fix" business model nearly 4 years ago, and which can be utilized by the SMB IT Service Provider as a resource in their quest for knowledge regarding Managed Services in general.

Make certain to register this book to download the over 30 forms, tools and collateral referenced herein and receive updates on tools, forms, information and other special offers at:

www.mspu.us/bookregistration

Preface

Intelligent Enterprise has been providing Information Technology solutions to the SMB market since 1997. Our relationships with Vendors and Fulfillment Partners have allowed us the ability to design, scale and implement effective infrastructure solutions for our diverse Client base.

In addition to providing Managed Services to our Clients, our Solution Stack includes Hosted Voice over IP Services, T1/Integrated T1 and Voice Services, Hosting and Co-Location Services, Application and Web Development and Wireless and Local and Wide-Area Networking, among others.

As a Microsoft Gold Certified Partner, Business Solutions Partner and Small Business Specialist, our Core Microsoft Competencies include Networking Infrastructure Solutions, Advanced Infrastructure Solutions and Information Worker Solutions.

We successfully migrated all of our existing Clients to a Managed Services delivery model in January of 2005. Prior to this, we operated as many other IT companies have – reacting to Client problems in "break-fix" mode, and dealing with the constant demand to recruit new Clients and sell new solutions each and every month to meet our receivables goals.

Our decision to move to a Managed Services delivery model was certainly not arbitrary. In fact, we viewed it as a Business Necessity, and the only way that we could remain competitive in our market without having to increase Staff. In our old "break-fix" business model, we were hampered by the necessity for Technicians to travel and provide on-site services. This directly impacted the amount of billing we could accomplish, as well as limited our utilization per Technician.

We now employ an "All You Can Eat" Remote Help Desk approach, along with 24x7x365 Network Monitoring services. Since developing our unique Managed Services Sales, Implementation and Maintenance programs, we have seen our monthly billing and utilization numbers *triple from previous years* without adding additional Staff. In fact, we have become so efficient, that *we now operate with less Staff*. And the best part? All of our Managed Services billing occurs in advance -

which for us is a welcome change from the way we used to bill in our old "break-fix" model – deliver services first, then bill afterwards and wait to get paid…and sometimes wait some more.

We sincerely believe that the Managed Services model has afforded us benefits that IT Service Providers in general will not be able to do long without. Among these is the recurring revenue that will continue to grow. The ability to project revenue and set revenue goals will become much easier. In addition, the Proactive nature of our Managed Services model has alleviated a tremendous burden from us - we now do much more with less, and can schedule and allocate resources for projects much more easily, as we are not reacting and fighting daily fires, but instead preventing them.

Perhaps the most significant benefit of our transition to a complete Managed Services model is the increasing value of our company as a whole. Based upon the nature and value of our Managed Services Agreements, we will be able to command a much higher sale price for our organization - when we choose to sell.

The value of these Managed Services Agreements can also be used to leverage Business Loans and Lines of Credit – options that are traditionally more difficult to execute when substantiated by a reactive "break-fix" or "time and materials" Service model.

What Can You Expect From This Book?

That is a good book which is opened with expectation and closed with profit.

Amos Bronson Alcott (1799 - 1888)

The purpose of this Book is threefold. First, we will define what "Managed Services" means to us, and what Core Services comprise our Managed Services deliverables.

Secondly, we will discuss the inherent benefits that delivering Managed Services can provide both to your organization, as well as your Clients - and how to structure your organization to deliver Managed Services.

Thirdly, we will illustrate a step-by-step process on how to transition your existing Clients to a Managed Services delivery model, close new Managed Services business, and evaluate your current Business, Technical and Sales and Marketing Processes to adjust them for compatibility with a Managed Services delivery model.

The Guide To A Successful Managed Services Practice

This book will reveal to you the nuts and bolts of our Managed Services deliverables – everything we do to sell, implement and maintain our Managed Services offering.

In addition, you will learn how we build Fulfillment-Partnering Relationships to deliver additional Annuity-Based Products and Services to our Client base, further increasing our monthly and yearly revenues.

The real value of this book lies in our unique Managed Services Concepts, and the Forms and Processes we have developed and utilize to deliver our successful Managed Services program.

We have included every single business form, tool and piece of marketing collateral that we utilize in our Managed Services practice as a download after registering this book at www.mspu.us/bookregistration. This includes 8 business forms, 12 different examples of direct mail, postcard and html email templates, and 4 PowerPoint sales presentations that you can brand and use in your own Managed Services practice. We have even included a sample Managed Services Agreement, as well as a detailed Help Desk Escalation Process for your review.

The Guide To A Successful Managed Services Practice

As a Special Bonus, we've also included our Microsoft TS2 Webcast: *"The Secret to a Successful Managed Services Business"*.

Whether you're a novice to the Managed Services concept, or a veteran who has already implemented some version of a Managed Services deliverable to your Client base, we are confident that you will gain a new perspective on the term "Managed Services" after reviewing the material contained in this book.

You will notice that throughout certain sections of this book, ideas and concepts are repeated, and may seem redundant.

This has been done intentionally, as there are those of you who may not read this book from start to finish, but instead jump directly to a specific chapter dealing with an item of immediate interest to you, or skip back and forth between chapters or sections.

Managed Services – What and Why?

I do not fear computers. I fear the lack of them.

Isaac Asimov (1920 - 1992)

It seems like the new buzz word that all of us in the IT Industry have been hearing for the last couple of years is "Managed Services". And doesn't it also seem that the definition of Managed Services changes depending upon whom you ask? In fact, this term is so new that you'll have a hard time finding a definition for it in the Dictionary!

Clear your mind for a moment of any existing preconceptions you might currently have about Managed Services, their definition, and anything else. Okay - ready?

For our purposes in the context of this material, let's assume the following definition for our Managed Services deliverables:

"Any defined set of Proactive Services that are Remotely Delivered and Prepaid For, on a Recurring Basis".

Let's digest our definition for a moment. The term "any" is a powerful one. It means just that – *any services*, not just network monitoring or IT Services in general. This is the reason that Hardware Vendors, Co-Location Facilities and Service Providers can all use the term "Managed Services" to describe their product or service.

Now let's look at the balance of the definition: *"Remotely-Delivered"*, *"Prepaid For"*, and especially – *"Recurring Basis"*.

By understanding these concepts, the SMB IT Service Provider can begin to appreciate how they can *increase their Technicians' and Engineers' utilization as well as their Revenue.*

The more services that can be delivered through remote means, the less frequently the need to schedule onsite visits, and the higher Labor Utilization grows. Earnings grow along with Labor Utilization. And the dread "feast or famine" cycles are eliminated over time, as existing Clients are transitioned, and new ones are added to the Managed Services model.

As monthly Earnings increase in this Annuity-Based service model, they will continue to grow exponentially each and every month.

Sounds good so far, right? Let's take it a step further. Now that we are delivering our Services through remote means, eliminating much of the travel time required for onsite support, and not trading time for money, we can do much more with less.

Think about it – travel is our biggest utilization killer. In our own local market, we can lose up to an hour traveling each way when providing onsite support. Add to that the reality that once a Technician or Engineer is onsite; he or she is typically only able to focus on resolving that one particular Client's problems.

So in this example, we've lost a couple of hours to travel, plus the onsite time. And we've addressed problems for only a single Client. Let's throw in a lunch hour for our Technician or

Engineer, since they haven't had one yet, and by the time they return to the office, they've potentially been gone for 6 hours (or more) – yikes! Plus - like most IT business owners, we're paying for the gasoline – and that's not getting any cheaper!

Now let's take the same example and address it through our Managed Services model. Instead of jumping in their car, our Technician or Engineer remotes in to the Client's network Server or end-user Desktop and initiates a maintenance or troubleshooting session. Let's say it's a basic cleanup and optimization task. Because there is generally not a lot going on while Antivirus scans are being run, drives are being defragmented, etc., our Technician or Engineer has the opportunity to address more than just this single issue for this particular Client.

In other words, *we are now able to address multiple issues remotely for different Clients concurrently.* Guess what that does for our utilization? That's right; we achieve utilization increases that are simply unattainable through the delivery of onsite support. Now let's be clear – not all issues can and will be resolved through remote means. But let's just say that *80%*

or more of them can be. *We've just netted real cost savings to our bottom line.*

Hold on – we're not done yet! We haven't yet explored the complete benefits of remote support, and you may be way ahead of me already. Now we can support many more Clients with the same amount (or less, as we found) of Staff. More real dollars to our bottom line! And who likes hiring, training and managing excess Staff?

In addition, through the implementation of a documented Help Desk SLA and Escalation Procedure (one that is consistently delivered by all Technicians and Engineers), we begin to eliminate some Clients' propensity to always request a specific Technician or Engineer to support them.

As the Client begins to realize that all issues are handled in exactly the same manner; and more quickly, as they are addressed by the next available Technician, rather than their "favorite" Technician, they will quickly become accustomed to this process. This eliminates billing bottlenecks for the SMB IT Service Provider, as they are not waiting for a specific Technician to resolve an issue before billing can occur.

Another point to consider is that with a Managed Services model, our Clients never haggle over our Invoices! How much time do you spend each month going over line items on Invoices with your existing Clients? Then negotiating *down* to keep them happy? Now all of our Flat-Fee Invoices go out in advance, and our Clients know what to expect each and every month, so we've eliminated Invoice Haggling!

Let's discuss for a moment the change in perception Managed Services Clients experience as a direct result of receiving Proactive Support. These Clients are now more likely to begin viewing the Managed Service Provider as much more than a "break-fix", reactive "computer guy", and more like a truly Proactive Advisor.

Let's face it – once we've quieted our Clients' networks down, we now have the opportunity – nay, *the responsibility* - to deliver Solutions to these Clients. As the Trusted Advisor, it is much easier to sell these Clients *Solutions*, as the value of our Services is elevated through the very nature of our Proactive Managed Services delivery model.

Now, as a result of our prepaid, long-term Annuity-Based Managed Services Agreements, we can logically expect the value of our organizations to increase. This is based directly upon the value and term of each of our individual Managed Services Agreements. We write three-year Managed Services Agreements, which automatically renew (some of our Partners write even longer terms into their Agreements – 5 years and beyond!). This has helped us significantly increase our organization's value, when compared with our old Month-to-Month block time/break-fix contracts.

We can now illustrate the following benefits to the Service Provider that is operating under a Managed Services model:

1. Realize the Benefits of an Annuity-based revenue model

2. Enjoy Long-Term Predictable revenue growth

3. Eliminate the Cycles of "*Feast or Famine*"

4. Bill Independently of Any Specific Technician

5. Stop Trading Time for Money

6. Do Much More with Less

      a. Remotely

      b. Proactively

      c. Dramatically reduce travel and associated expenses

7. Eliminate Invoice haggling

8. Sell Solutions Much More Easily

9. Increase Your Valuation!

This all makes perfect sense for the Managed Service Provider, but what benefits can the Managed Service Provider's Clients expect from this Proactive model?

Well, there are many – beginning with Increased Operational Efficiency. Let's face it – a well maintained, Proactively-serviced network and its devices will always run better than the alternative. With Proactive Network Monitoring, Patch Management and Device Optimization being performed on a regular basis, Clients will notice a tremendously positive difference. They will now benefit as we spend our time preventing fires, rather than fighting them.

These Managed Services Clients will now be able to control and reduce their overall operating costs as a benefit of the Flat-Fee billing model, and budget these costs much more easily.

Cost-effective access to Enterprise-level support now truly becomes a reality for Managed Services Clients, as we escalate Tier 3 problems and above to Vendors, and enlist their assistance in resolving even the most complex issues. This type of support is covered under all of our Managed Services Agreements.

Minimized downtime is a logical byproduct of a well-designed and effectively executed Managed Services maintenance program as well.

And because we also manage all of our Clients' Infrastructure Vendor relationships, they are now able to focus on running their Businesses, not their Vendors. As a result of our "Always Eyes-On" status of monitoring their networks 24 hours a day, our Clients experience an additional level of comfort and security.

The following list details the benefits to the Client that is covered under a Managed Services Agreement:

1. Benefit from Increased Operational Efficiency

2. Reduce and Control Their Operating Costs

3. Cost-effectively gain access to Enterprise-level Support

4. Experience Minimized Downtime

5. Able to focus on running their Business, not their Vendors

6. Receive piece of mind, with the knowledge that their environment is being monitored 24/7/365

Incidentally, these are key areas to always highlight during Sales Presentations with Prospective Clients.

Why Transition to a Managed Services Delivery Model Now?

If we don't change direction soon, we'll end up where we're going.

Professor Irwin Cory (1914 -)

According to Gartner, *"the fastest growing part of the IT Management Market is the Remote Operation and Management of Networks and IT Infrastructure"**

and…

"the Remote Monitoring and Management market is expected to grow at a compound annual growth rate of 36 percent through 2008".*

Numerous Industry Experts concur in the identification of the IT Industry's shift towards increasing adoption of the Managed

---

* Publication Date: January 3rd, 2005

Services Delivery model. If the SMB IT Service Provider doesn't begin to move their Client base over to Proactively Managed Services over the next twelve to eighteen months, Analysts predict that their Managed Services competitors will begin to erode this base.

As more and more large players in the IT Product and Services sector adopt a Managed Services delivery and support model, many SMB IT Providers may feel left, or squeezed out of this increasingly competitive market.

With the rising acceptance of this paradigm shift to Proactive Service Delivery, the traditional "break-fix" or "block-time" model will become increasingly less appealing to the end-user Client - especially as they begin to receive messaging from more and more Vendors and Providers highlighting the benefits available through the Managed Services model.

It is a commonly shared belief by many in the Managed Services sector that commoditization of these Services is inevitable, and price wars will follow soon afterwards. This is why it is critical to the SMB IT Service Provider to move quickly to transition to Managed Services, and build market share with solid Client Relationships, in order to remain competitive in the future.

How the Managed Services Model Affects Valuation

The wise man is he who knows the relative value of things.

William Ralph Inge (1860 - 1954)

Do you own a business, or own a job?

job[1]

n.

1. A regular activity performed in exchange for payment, especially as one's trade, occupation, or profession.

2. A position in which one is employed.

What's the primary reason you decided to start and run your own business? Was it because you thought that by being your own boss, you would have greater freedom, command respect and become wealthy? Pretty much mirrors most people's idea of Success, doesn't it?

What's the reality? Working long hours, reacting to Client needs, never being able to take the time off that you originally dreamed of? And what about the other side of the business – *actually running the business?*

If you're like most of us, you're good at either being an Engineer, great at customer service, an excellent salesperson or a first-rate business owner operationally (on top of finances, projections, human resources, taxes and the rest). Very seldom do we find individuals that are experienced and excel in every single area required to operate and build a successful business.

The good news is that we can find the people that we need to complement us in the areas we need help with. These folks do exist – *so what do we do when we find them? Does simply bringing them in increase the value of our businesses?* Maybe… *and maybe not.*

The key to maximizing the value of an organization is in maximizing consistent Earnings over time.

How can a break-fix company accurately forecast future Earnings? They really can't, can they? But an Annuity-Based Managed Services model easily allows us the ability to forecast Earnings.

Industry statistics reflect that the value of an IT company employing the traditional reactive "break-fix" model may be less than 1x its Earnings.

So for example, a traditional "break-fix" IT company with Earnings of $50,000 per month in Services alone would be worth $600,000 at a 1x Earnings Valuation ($50,000 x 12 months x 1). This value; by itself, would not be a powerful motivator to sell, as the company could simply continue to operate and earn identical returns the following year.

Now let's take the same exact company, but transform their $50,000 Earnings per month to Annuity-Based revenue through the Managed Services model. In this case, Industry Statistics show that as high as a 10x Earnings Valuation may be possible with Goodwill. This means that this same exact company could possibly be worth $6 Million dollars ($50,000 x 12 months x 10) over time. *Even if other factors reduce this*

Valuation by 50%, this still remains an extremely powerful motivator for the decision to transition to Managed Services.

Please note that we're speaking of Earnings here, not Gross Revenue. Only you know how much Gross Revenue you will need to generate in order to achieve Earnings of $50,000 per month – adjust your projections accordingly.

Another point to consider for those business owners that aren't ready to sell, but would instead like to expand their organizations, is that the same criteria for Valuation can apply when applying for Business Loans or Lines of Credit. Annuity-Based Service Agreements will always be worth more than "block-time" Service Agreements – and the longer the Term, the higher their value.

Be advised of the obvious here - these numbers and formulas are not hard and fast rules. Business Valuation can be determined through many methods, or a combination of different methods including:

- Book Value

- Adjusted Book Value (Tangible or Economic)

- Income Capitalization

- Discounted Earnings

- Discounted Cash Flow

- Price Earnings Multiples

- Dividend Capitalization

- Sales Multiple

- Profit Multiple

- Liquidation Value

- Replacement Value

- True Value

The key point to remember here is that the "real world" or "Fair Market" value of your organization will be the ultimate amount that a buyer is willing to pay you for it at time of sale. It stands to reason that a buyer would be willing to pay a much higher premium for your organization based on Projected Earnings from your Annuity-Based Service Agreements, than they would from your historical "break-fix" or "block-time" revenue.

A great website to visit to begin learning about business valuation is Score's business valuation page:

http://www.score.org/article_business_valuation_101.html

So what is your Exit Strategy? We're told that every Business Owner needs to be clear on his or her Exit Strategy, which drives their Business and Marketing Plans. Let's take a hypothetical example.

Let's say that your Exit Strategy is based upon retiring early, and that means within the next 5 years. And let's assume that your financial planning projections indicate that you would need $5 Million dollars, with the proper returns, for you to provide for your family and live comfortably the rest of your life.

A widely accepted method used to determine what your company's consistent Earnings would need to be to sell for $5 Million dollars is to employ *Reverse Projection*. For this example, we'll assume that you will be able to achieve a 5x Earnings Valuation of your company prior to sale.

So the formula we'll employ is a simple mathematical equation:

Target Amount ÷ Desired Earnings Valuation ÷ 12 = Monthly Earnings

Since our Target Amount is $5MM, we would divide that by 5 (our desired Earnings Valuation), which gives us $1MM. We now divide $1MM by 12 months, and end up with about $83,333 and change.

This means that you would need consistent Earnings of roughly $83,333 per month, over time, to achieve a $5 Million dollar Valuation ($83,333 x 12 months x 5). This type of forecasting is critical, if you are to accomplish your Exit Strategy, and will stimulate you to modify your business plan, marketing plan, deliverables, expectations, or all of the above.

We can easily demonstrate the ability to achieve these Monthly Earnings in several ways:

1. Sell 83 Clients a Managed Services Plan at $1,000/month

2. Sell 42 Clients a Managed Services Plan at $2,000/month

3. Sell Any Number of Clients additional Annuity-based Services at $$/month

4. Any combination of the above – be creative!

Remember – we're talking about <u>*Earnings*</u> *here, not Gross Revenue. You'll need to determine what your actual Gross Revenue would need to be per month in order to meet your specific Earnings goals.*

That's the basic idea. Once you understand what will be required of you, determine what it's going to take, and build an Annuity-based Managed Services program around it.

Did you notice that your 5-Year Retirement Timeline did not figure into these reverse projections? That's because *you drive how quickly or slowly you reach your Earnings goal* – if you're really motivated, you might get there sooner!

Also note that you will obviously sell and implement services that are not always Annuity-Based. The best example of these is the PROJECT. By all means, sell Projects – just realize that historical Project revenue will not have as significant an impact on the Value of your company as Annuity-Based Revenue will (but it's great revenue just the same!).

Also keep this in mind – Managed Services is only 1 Component in a well-rounded Annuity-Based Service Delivery Model...

Managed Services Deliverables

Great services are not canceled by one act or by one single error.

Benjamin Disraeli (1804 - 1881)

In keeping with our focus on Managed Services as being only a single component within the larger scope of a completely well-rounded Annuity-based IT Service Delivery Model, let's identify three Value-Added services that comprise a "killer" Managed Services offering:

1. Network Monitoring

2. Remote Help Desk

3. Vendor Management

Network Monitoring

With the advent of the ability for Server and Desktop Operating Systems, Critical Services and other Network Devices such as Printers, Routers and Firewalls to output events through WMI, SNMP and Syslogs, numerous monitoring tools and services have surfaced from companies such as Kaseya, Level Platforms, N-Able, Nagios, Silverback, Zenith Infotech and others.

While all network monitoring tools share some commonality – the ability to monitor basic Events, and customize and trigger Alerts, for example - each has its own Pros and Cons.

When evaluating a Network Monitoring Tool or Service, it's important to make certain that it performs basic functions such as:

- WMI Monitoring

- Syslog Monitoring

- SNMP Monitoring

- Alerting – Email/Text Page/Pager

- Has Configurable Alerts

- Supports Escalation

- Provides Meaningful Reporting

- Outputs Detailed Logging

- Supports Multiple Operating Systems

- Supports Critical Server Functions – Exchange/SQL/IIS/SharePoint/Linux/Novell

- Supports Multiple Types of Hardware –
  PC's/Servers/Routers/Switches/Firewalls/Printers

- Supports Multiple 3rd-Party Software Monitoring

- Supports Patch Management

- Easily Integrates With Help Desk Systems

- Supports Remote Control of Monitored Devices

- Is Affordable – Able to Monitor Numerous Devices
  Cost-Effectively

- Is easy to Install, Deploy, Use and Maintain

- Has excellent Vendor Support – and during the hours
  that your organization operates

Here are the URL's of some popular Network Monitoring Tools to review:

Handsfree Networks

www.handsfreenetworks.com

HoundDog

www.hounddogiseasy.com

HyBlue

www.hyblue.com

ITControlSuite

www.itcontrolsuite.com

Kaseya

www.kaseya.com

LabTech Software

www.labtechsoft.com

Level Platforms

www.levelplatforms.com

N-able

www.n-able.com

Nagios

www.nagios.org

Secure My Company

www.securemycompany.com

Silverback Technologies (Dell)

www.silverbacktech.com

VirtualAdministrator

www.virtualadministrator.com

Zenith Infotech

www.zenithinfotech.com

We utilize network monitoring tools for the same basic purpose – providing Proactive Alerting of problems that can affect the normal operation of a critical Device or Service. For instance, wouldn't you like to know when CPU utilization is high on a SQL Server, and for how long? How about receiving an Alert when Disk Space has dropped below a specific threshold? Or when a Backup Job has failed? Or if the Exchange Information Store Service has stopped? Or if a VPN connection has dropped? Or a Website or Web Server is down?

All of these alerts can positively impact a Client's uptime, if received and dealt with in a timely manner. These tools can basically monitor virtually every Windows and many other Operating Systems' Events generated, as well as specific Network Hardware Events, and 3rd Party Software Events – like Virus Alerts, and Update and Service Pack alerting. Some of them even have the ability to automatically restart stalled or failed Services – *what a time-saver, and added value for you and your Clients!* If you support environments other than Windows, you'll obviously need to choose a tool that will allow you to monitor those particular systems as well.

And the best part about these monitoring tools?

They work 24 hours a day, 7 days a week, and 365 days a year, never get sick, come in late, or take a day off.

Our Monitoring System is configured to automatically restart Critical Services, should they fail. It is also set to automatically create Trouble Tickets in our Help Desk Systems for Critical Alerts, or when the restart of Critical Services has failed.

Our Help Desk Technicians actively manage both our Monitoring System Console, as well as our Help Desk Service Board.

What to Monitor

So what should you monitor? Logic dictates that any Critical Device or Service in your Clients' environments should be Proactively Monitored, after setting appropriate thresholds. You can find out what these thresholds should be by contacting the appropriate Vendor for their Best Practices data, whether the data is for Server Operating Systems, Managed Firewalls, Routers, or other Devices, Systems and Services.

From a Server perspective, there are obvious Services to keep an eye on. The following list in now way should be viewed as comprehensive – in fact it is far from it. It is included simply to give you something to think about, as you explore the vastness that comprises Network Monitoring in general, and prepare yourself for the journey that lies ahead:

- Memory Utilization

- Available Memory

- Utilized Disk Space

- Available Disk Space

- CPU Load

- Utilized Paging File

- Available Paging File

- Print Spooler Service

- Printing Events

- DHCP Service and Events

- IIS Service and Events

- DNS Service and Events

- RRAS Services and Events

- Terminal Services and Events

- SQL Services and Events

- Informational Security Events

- Critical Security Events

- Informational System Events

- Critical System Events

- Uninterruptible Power Supply Events

- Backup Events

Remote Help Desk

We touched on the benefits of providing service to Clients through remote means earlier. Here's where we kick it up a notch. An efficient Help Desk is a beautiful thing. With a well-trained Staff and a solid SLA and Escalation Process, your Help Desk is your company's best representation of value to your Clients. If your Help Desk is inefficient, your Clients will suffer, and you will lose them. If your Help Desk is World-Class, your Clients will continue to utilize your Services, and will be happy to refer you more business, be open to more Solutions, or participate in Testimonials – or all three.

Our Help Desk provides Unlimited Remote Support between the hours of 8am and 5pm Monday through Friday, across 4 Time Zones to our Clients, as well as our Managed Services Partners' Clients, with all Services included in their monthly fee. That's right – *Unlimited Remote Support*. We've found that Clients appreciate being able to budget their IT costs for the entire year, knowing that there will be no unreasonable fluctuations.

So what do we provide to our Direct Clients?

Help Desk

1. Unlimited Remote, Onsite and Lab/Bench Time Support 8am-5pm M-F

   a. Some Specific Limitations

   b. Phone Support

   c. Remote Desktop Control

2. 5pm-9pm Billable @ 1.5x

3. All Other Times Billable @ 2x

4. Server Disaster Recovery Included as needed

You'll notice that there are *some specific limitations*. So what does that mean? Well, that covers us in situations where a new Client has some Line of Business Software or 3rd Party piece of equipment that we've never run into, had training on, etc. We will normally disclaim including that software or device in our initial Service Agreement. But that doesn't mean we'll never support it – we perform our due diligence with the

Vendor of the software or piece of equipment in question, in order to evaluate their support, how easy it is to contact them, and what they will or will not do. If there is training available, we will get trained. We may end up including support for this software or piece of equipment in our Agreement, or raise our fee in order to include support, or not provide direct support, but simply manage the Vendor when Vendor support is needed. But in most cases, *we provide some level of support between the Client and the Vendor.*

A recent example which illustrates this scenario involves a Client we signed to a Managed Services Agreement with 35 Desktops and 2 Servers. They provide power management solutions to large Malls and Retail Stores. In addition to our normally-supported software applications, they asked us to support 3 additional software applications that allow them to monitor and report on power usage at their Client's locations.

Since we had no experience with these 3 software applications, or their Vendors, we initially excluded this support from their Flat-Fee Managed Services Agreement, and billed directly for all support on these applications for a period of 3 months. After this time, we were familiar enough with these applications, and, more importantly, what we could expect as far as Vendor support, to renegotiate our Flat-Fee Managed Services Agreement with our Client, and increase it by $500 per month to include support for these unfamiliar software applications.

You can get an idea of our standard inclusions and exclusions for Support by reviewing Appendix B of the Sample Managed Services Agreement included with the downloads available after registering this book at www.mspu.us/bookregistration.

So we obviously provide Phone, Remote, Onsite and Lab/Bench Time support. But what happens after 5pm, do we just shut down? No, we continue to provide support 24/7/365 - if the Client chooses to pay for it. Between the hours of 5pm and 9pm, our fee is time and a half, and any time after that, it's double. You'd be amazed at how many requests for after-hours support we've stopped receiving since implementing this rate plan!

As indicated, we include Onsite and Lab/Bench Time Services in our Flat-Rate All-You-Can Eat pricing model between the hours of 8am-5pm M-F - as well as Server Disaster Recovery. You might initially think this is crazy – until we explain the reasoning behind it.

You see, we only go onsite (from a Trouble-Ticket perspective) when there is a physical Hardware Failure, or other extraordinary reason. So by including all Onsite Visits and Lab/Bench Time in our Service Agreements, we are not necessarily required to go onsite any more often than we would otherwise. This is a tremendous psychological Sales tool, as the Client loves the idea that their monthly fee will not fluctuate, no matter how and where Services are delivered.

This is also true for including Disaster Recovery of Servers in our Service Agreements. Let's face it – if the Client's Server is being properly maintained, and Proactively Monitored, we're not likely to see a failure requiring a complete Recovery. So the "All-You-Can Eat" Remote, Onsite and Lab/Bench Time Help Desk Service, with Server Disaster Recovery included in our Flat-Fee Service Agreements, provide us a tremendously powerful Unique Selling Proposition with Prospective Clients – differentiating ourselves from all of the Service Providers we have competed against to win Client Business.

With the exclusion of Server Disaster Recovery; which is not billable at anytime it is delivered, our Lab/Bench Time and Onsite Rates (for those times when we absolutely, positively have to be there) are billable at 1.5x established Rates between 5pm and 9pm and 2x thereafter.

One of the policies we've also instituted which has continued to reduce our need to travel onsite, is the requirement for all of our Clients to purchase an additional PC (or more, depending on the size of their environment) as a spare. We have it configured and stored away somewhere at their location, so that if a user's PC fails, they simply hook up the spare, we remote into it and configure the user's profile, and they're back to work.

Think about it – on the right day, and for a few hundred bucks, your Client can get a decent Dell PC with the appropriate Operating System preinstalled. In our market, by the time we're done driving over and servicing their failed PC (or verifying that it's dead and needs parts to be replaced), it's going to cost our Client at least that much – so the spare PC just makes sense. Plus this way, when you need parts, you're not out of luck – Dell's got tons of them, and you can get them the next day.

After the user is back to work, we let the Client know that the next time we're in the area, we'll pick up the failed PC and work on it <u>IN OUR LAB</u>. Remember – keep utilization high by performing as many services in your offices as possible. Our Technicians and Engineers always have multiple Lab projects going, so they can multi-task and book their Utilization time against several Client accounts concurrently.

Oh – I almost forgot. Clients can't just get our Remote Help Desk (or our Managed Services Program in general) just because they see the value and want it really, really badly. They've got to qualify - not only with their environment, but also *with their attitude.*

Did that sound a bit strange – I mean the "attitude" part? Okay, let's get into it - environment first. In order for our Client's environment to qualify for Managed Services, there are minimum infrastructure requirements that have to be met:

- All Servers with Microsoft Operating Systems must be running Windows Server 2003 or SBS2003 or later, and have all of the latest Microsoft Service Packs and Critical Updates installed. Non-Microsoft Servers must meet similar OS-Specific requirements.

- All Desktop PC's and Notebooks/Laptops with Microsoft Operating Systems must be running Windows XP Pro or later, and have all of the latest Microsoft Service Packs and Critical Updates installed. All Non-Microsoft PC's and Notebooks/Laptops must meet similar OS-Specific requirements.

- All Server and Desktop Software must be Genuine, Licensed and Vendor-Supported.

- The environment must have a currently licensed, up-to-date and Vendor-Supported Server-based Antivirus Solution protecting all Servers, Desktops, Notebooks/Laptops, and Email.

- The environment must have a currently licensed, up-to-date and Vendor-Supported Anti-Spam Solution.

- The environment must have a currently licensed, Vendor-Supported Server or Network-based Backup Solution.

- The environment must have a currently licensed, Vendor-Supported Firewall between the Internal Network and the Internet.

- All Wireless data traffic in the environment must be securely encrypted.

- The environment must have a T1 or other form of High-Speed Internet Access with Static IP's.

- The environment must contain Spare PC(s)

The Client is billed to bring the environment up to these minimum "Certified Network" standards.

So we basically need an infrastructure that we can monitor, support and remote in to. This makes our requirements for Server and Desktop Operating Systems easy. However; we happen to be very picky about the Antivirus, Anti-Spam, Backup and Network Monitoring Solutions we use. You can obviously use whatever you feel provides the best features and functionality, as well as excellent Vendor support.

That all makes sense, right? Well, what about that "attitude" thing? Maybe more than anything else, we feel that in order for someone to become and remain our Client, we need to be able to sell them SOLUTIONS.

Think about it – if you can't sell your Client Solutions, then they don't properly perceive the value of your relationship with them. You need to either change their perception of your relationship (we'll talk about this later), or find a new Client. Deep down you know that you're going to spend more time trying to keep a "C" Clients (that don't "get it") happy, than you will your "A" Clients.

What's worse than that? Watch this:

The revenue that you lose dealing with "C" Clients can't be compared to <u>the time that they rob</u> you from spending with your "A" Clients.

Think about that one for a moment…

What's your definition of "A", "B", and "C" Clients? See if it differs significantly from ours:

"A" Clients:	"B" Clients:	"C" Clients:
Pay On Time – or ahead of time	May Experience Some Payment Issues	Slow Pay
Have IT Budgets	Have Limited Budgets	No Budget
Allow Direct Access to Decision Makers	May Not Allow Direct Access To Decision Makers	Does it matter?

Help Desk Best Practices

What are the goals of a successful Help Desk? They should include:

- Provide a single point of contact for end-user issues

- Facilitate the restoration of normal service operation while minimizing impact to the end-user

- Deliver services within agreed-upon SLA's

What are the duties of a successful Help Desk? They should include:

- **Receive all incident notifications** – this can be through any means - phone, fax or Email

- **Record all incidents** – this must be accomplished with a robust, searchable incident tracking system

- **Classify all incidents** – correctly document the nature of the incident, including affected users, systems, hardware and services

- **Prioritize all incidents** – proper prioritization is essential to effective escalation

- **Troubleshoot all incidents** – perform established troubleshooting procedures according to manufacturer's and vendor's best practices

- **Escalate all incidents as necessary** – proper escalation insures adherence to established SLA's (this includes escalation to 3rd-Party Vendors for Support)

- **Maintain consistent communication with all parties** – including end-users, their managers and higher, as well as your own internal Help Desk Management hierarchy

- **Perform all scheduled activities** – moves/adds/changes, maintenance, patch management, documentation and reporting

- **Prepare and brief reports to Help Desk Management and/or Clients on Help Desk performance**

In order to maintain a successful Help Desk, Internal Objectives need to be clear, Client requirements and SLA's documented and understood, and training for Help Desk Staff *as well as Clients* needs to be conducted regularly. Help Desk deliverables need to be clearly defined and Service Levels monitored regularly, and modified as needed. Here is an example of a clearly-defined Response, Resolution and Escalation Time SLA:

Trouble	Priority	Response time (in hours) *	Resolution time (in hours) *	Escalation threshold (in hours)
Service not available (all users and functions unavailable).	1	Within 1 hour	ASAP – Best Effort	2 hours
Significant degradation of service (large number of users or business critical functions affected)	2	Within 4 hours	ASAP – Best Effort	4 hours
Limited degradation of service (limited number of users or functions affected, business process can continue).	3	Within 24 hours	ASAP – Best Effort	48 hours
Small service degradation (business process can continue, one user affected).	4	within 48 hours	ASAP – Best Effort	96 hours

It is also important to identify and document Help Desk Support Tiers. Providing this information to the Client assists tremendously in setting the appropriate expectation with all Parties. Review the following Support Tier example:

Support Tier	Description
Tier 1 Support	All support incidents begin in Tier 1, where the initial trouble ticket is created, the issue is identified and clearly documented, and basic hardware/software troubleshooting is initiated.
Tier 2 Support	All support incidents that cannot be resolved with Tier 1 Support are escalated to Tier 2, where more complex support on hardware/software issues can be provided by more experienced Engineers.
Tier 3 Support	Support Incidents that cannot be resolved by Tier 2 Support are escalated to Tier 3, where support is provided by the most qualified and experienced Engineers who have the ability to collaborate with 3rd Party (Vendor) Support Engineers to resolve the most complex issues.

One of the most important components of a well-run Help Desk is a clearly-defined Escalation Process. Without one, every Technician will be handling tickets in their own manner, and in most cases – inconsistently. This is especially true between several Technicians, and can quickly negatively skew the end-user's perception of the Help Desk's Internal Process, as Trouble Ticket requests are handled and Escalated (or not!) differently each time they are opened. The following is a simple, easy to implement and maintain Help Desk Escalation Process:

Service Request Escalation Procedure

1. Support Request is Received
2. Trouble Ticket is Created
3. Issue is Identified and documented in Help Desk system
4. Issue is qualified to determine if it can be resolved through Tier 1 Support

If issue can be resolved through Tier 1 Support:

5. Level 1 Resolution - issue is worked to successful resolution
6. Quality Control - Issue is verified to be resolved to Client's satisfaction
7. Trouble Ticket is closed, after complete problem resolution details have been updated in Help Desk system

If issue cannot be resolved through Tier 1 Support:

6. Issue is escalated to Tier 2 Support
7. Issue is qualified to determine if it can be resolved by Tier 2 Support

If issue can be resolved through Tier 2 Support:

8. Level 2 Resolution - issue is worked to successful resolution
9. Quality Control - Issue is verified to be resolved to Client's satisfaction

10. Trouble Ticket is closed, after complete problem resolution details have been updated in Help Desk system

If issue cannot be resolved through Tier 2 Support:

9. Issue is escalated to Tier 3 Support
10. Issue is qualified to determine if it can be resolved through Tier 3 Support

If issue can be resolved through Tier 3 Support:

11. Level 3 Resolution - issue is worked to successful resolution
12. Quality Control - Issue is verified to be resolved to Client's satisfaction
13. Trouble Ticket is closed, after complete problem resolution details have been updated in Help Desk system

If issue cannot be resolved through Tier 3 Support:

12. Issue is escalated to Onsite Support
13. Issue is qualified to determine if it can be resolved through Onsite Support

If issue can be resolved through Onsite Support:

14. Onsite Resolution - issue is worked to successful resolution
15. Quality Control - Issue is verified to be resolved to Client's satisfaction

16. Trouble Ticket is closed, after complete problem resolution details have been updated in Help Desk system

If issue cannot be resolved through Onsite Support:

17. IT Manager Decision Point – request is updated with complete details of all activity performed

The following is a graphical illustration of the Help Desk Escalation Process described above (this illustration is also available with the downloads available after registering this book at www.mspu.us/bookregistration).

HELP DESK SERVICE CALL ROUTING PROCESS

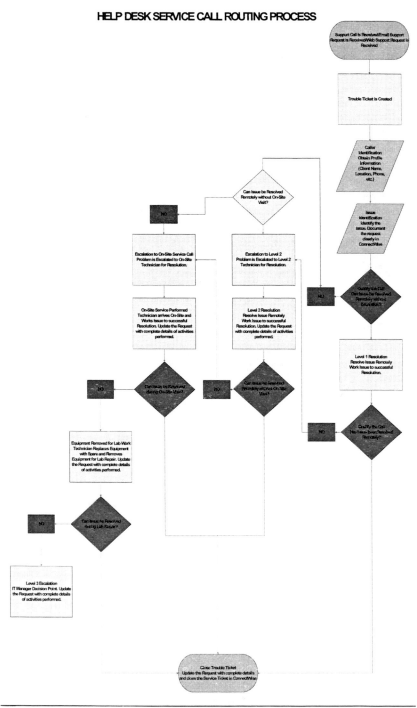

One key component of a successful Help Desk, besides an established, effective Operational and Escalation process, is the quality of its Staff. It's vitally important to insure the correct balance of Tier 1, Tier 2 and Tier 3-Skilled Support Staff. The correct balance of Skill Sets can make the difference between meeting your SLA's, and losing Clients.

So some of the requirements necessary to operate a successful Help Desk include:

1. The right amount of Staff with the appropriate Skill Sets

2. Documented Operational and Escalation Procedures – for both Help Desk Staff and End-User Clients

3. Ongoing training – both for Staff and End-User Clients

4. Effective Help Desk Tools

There are numerous resources available on the Internet and elsewhere to research Help Desk methodology in tremendous detail, but let's take a minute to discuss Incident Tracking tools. Our experience in this area has allowed us the opportunity to use many of the most popular Help Desk software packages available, and we'd like to point out a few tips on what to look for when researching these tools.

When evaluating Help Desk software packages, here are a few things to look for:

- The ability to automatically receive Trouble Ticket requests via Email

- The ability to automatically Classify and Prioritize Incidents based upon keywords in Email Subject or Body

- The ability to configure automatic Escalation based on either severity, elapsed time, assigned Staff, or any combination of the above

- The ability to perform multiple means of Alerting – Email, Text Messaging, Paging, etc.

- The ability to easily allow Staff to Create, Update, Escalate and communicate Incidents and Status

- Ease of Customization – especially in the areas of Time Tracking, Escalation, Alerting and Billing

- Excellent Vendor Support – especially during your hours of operation

- Support for your Tax Rates – especially if outside of the United States

- Ease of Operation and Maintenance

- The ability to easily and automatically communicate status to end-users, Clients or Internal Staff from within the system as Service Requests are received, and as Status changes occur

- The ability to track Assets, Inventory and Licensing

- The ability to output Network Diagrams of supported environments

- The ability to track all Client and End-User information

- The ability to provide Remote Assistance from within the system itself

- Meaningful reporting capabilities – track tickets opened/closed, time to close, summary and detail, utilization, etc

- The ability to access the system securely from the Internet – great for closing Incidents when Onsite

- The ability to easily integrate with Network Monitoring Systems

- The ability to easily integrate with Accounting Systems

- Affordability

Obviously, this list could go on and on. You'll easily be able to compare the top 5 Help Desk Software applications head-to-head – they are all rich on features. Some are much more expensive than others – you'll need to decide what works best for you.

Here's a short list of some popular Help Desk Application Vendors for your review, please Google "Help Desk Software" for more:

Autotask

www.autotask.com

ConnectWise

www.connectwise.com

Frontrange Solutions

www.frontrange.com

Kemma Software

www.kemma.com

GWI Software

www.gwi.com

Helpstar

www.helpstar.com.

NetHelpDesk

www.nethelpdesk.com

Novo Solutions

www.novosolutions.com

Results Software

www.results-software.com

Shockey Monkey

www.shockeymonkey.com

Tigerpaw Software

www.tigerpawsoftware.com

Vendor Management

Ah – the Crowd Pleaser. Just what is Vendor Management? Basically, it's just what it sounds like – we manage the Client's Vendors. *All of them*. Every single one. Okay, maybe not *every* one – but the Infrastructure ones that matter:

- **Telco/Long Distance/Teleconferencing** – SBC/ATT/Bell/Verizon/Sprint/All Others

- **Broadband** – SBC/TelePacific/XO/MPower/All Others

- **Network Fax/Copier/Printer** – Xerox/Toshiba/Panasonic/Minolta/HP/All Others

- **Web/Dev/Database** – Webmasters/Developers/All Others

- **Line Of Business Software** – AccPac/Legal Solutions/TimeSlips/Quickbooks/Point/All Others

- **Hosting/Co-Lo** – Web Host/Co-Location Facility/All Others

- **Equipment** – Dell/HP/IBM/Cisco/All Others

- **Point Of Sale** – Keystroke/MS Retail Management System/All Others

- **Phone System** – Avaya/Lucent/Nortel/Panasonic/VoIP/All Others

- **Local Phone System Service Company** – All

Why in the world would we do this? It just sounds like a big headache, doesn't it? Well, frankly – it is! But think of it another way for a minute – ready?

You're already supporting your Client's Vendor relationships anyway.

Let me say that again:

You're already supporting your Client's Vendor relationships anyway. <u>You're probably just not getting paid to do it!</u>

I'll prove it to you – just think back to the last time you got a call from:

1) *One of your Client's Vendors, who happened to be Onsite… and was getting ready to do something you knew nothing about… and weren't exactly prepared to deal with at that exact moment… and they needed your help (or the Administrator password!) right now!*

Or…

2) *your Client, who had been working with one of his Vendors to (pick one):*

   a) *Install some upgrade or another and was having some difficulty (or screwed something up!)*

   or…

   b) *Was finalizing an order for a piece of equipment or software with a Vendor that he didn't need, or wouldn't integrate into the environment*

   or…

c) *Had already ordered and received a piece of equipment or software from a Vendor that he didn't need, or wouldn't integrate into the environment, and the Vendor was onsite to install it and needed your help*

or...

d) *You fill it in…..*

Get the picture? I know you're silently nodding your head up and down right now! My favorite one is the (pick one) DSL Provider, T1 Provider, Phone System Provider, or Network Copier Provider that requires you to drop what you're doing, meet them onsite right now, and *show them how to do their job* – good times!

Okay, so we've established that no matter how *Proactive* your Managed Services are, your Client's Vendors will cause you to become Reactive every time. And to top it off, you'll have a tough time getting your Client to pay you in these situations ("Well, I don't understand – how come I'm paying (*insert vendor name here*) and you too for the same thing?") That's just not right, now is it?

All of these reasons, and more, are why we created Vendor Management.

Vendor Management, the Client and You

Okay, how exactly does Vendor Management Work? In broad strokes, we basically list all of our Client's Vendors on our Managed Services Vendor Management Form*. This form lists each Vendor's contact information, Client's account number, last date of service and other necessary information. After merging this information onto our Managed Services Letter of Agency*, and printing it on the Client's Letterhead, we have them sign it. We then mail/fax it to the Vendor, taking the first step in assuming authority over the Client's Vendor account.

So what does that do for us? Absolutely Nothing – *if that's all we do*. But now the fun starts. We add value for the Client by taking care of all situations relating to any of their Vendors, relieving the Client from dealing with issues that we can resolve more quickly, and allowing them to focus on running their business – not their Vendors.

This all seems very valuable for the Client, agreed? Now – other than allowing us to be Proactive with Vendors, here's where it's also valuable for us – if we have an issue with any of

---

* *Included as a download*

the Client's Vendors (bad support, poor response, etc.), or can save the Client money, we will bring in one of our own *Preferred Vendors*.

What is a "Preferred Vendor"? A Vendor that we have a long-standing, trusted relationship with, who performs their services flawlessly, *and who pays us a commission for bringing them into a new Relationship, as well as an Annuity for each of their Solutions every month.*

These types of Relationships are the key to growing your Annuity-Based Revenues far beyond simply providing Managed Services and occasional Projects to your Clients, and help you reach your Exit Strategy more quickly.

Now, let's be clear on a key point. In no way whatsoever does the Client ever suffer from bringing in a Preferred Vendor. What I mean to say is – all of our Vendors' pricing must be competitive with any other Vendor's offering, and any commissions we receive must not impact what the Client pays – they come directly from the Vendor to us, in much the same way as any of the myriad Vendor "Influencer", "Agent" or "Reseller" Programs that exist today compensate their Channel Partners.

In most instances, our Clients understand these relationships, and would rather see us receive any additional commissions for bringing them the Solutions they need, rather than an outside Sales Rep whom they may never see again after the sale is complete.

Okay, so what other benefits does Vendor Management offer? For one, it continues to build the relationship between you and your Clients, and helps differentiate you from all of the "other" IT companies out there competing for your Clients' business.

Think about this – how difficult would it be for another IT company providing only "break-fix" services to take your Clients' accounts from you, if you're providing:

Managed Services

1. 24x7x365 Network Monitoring

2. "All-You-Can Eat" Help Desk

3. Vendor Management

All for one fixed, monthly fee?

Are You a Fan Yet?

What you risk reveals what you value. -
Jeanette Winterson

By now I hope you've become a fan of the Proactive Managed IT Services Delivery model, and if you're not, well there's a well-known saying I'm certain you're familiar with:

Not everybody gets it.

But there's another lesser-known part to this saying that follows:

Those that don't will be surpassed by those that do.

Unfortunately, it's the same for your Clients. Not all of them will get it. But guess what? That's actually a *good thing*. If you choose to make the transition to a Managed Services model, don't spend a lot of time trying to make your "C" Clients "get it".

There are too many "A" Client Prospects out there for you to approach.

In fact, I'll make you a bet. I'll bet that if you follow the methodologies in this book, and use the forms included with the downloads available after registering this book at www.mspu.us/bookregistration properly, you'll be surprised at how easy it is to sell Managed Services.

Now, for you skeptics out there, - those of you that have tried selling *Network Monitoring* as *Managed Services* and have experienced less than stellar results - pay special attention...

You see, we also tried selling Network Monitoring as a Stand-Alone service, when we were first getting our noses bloodied developing our Managed Services program. We demo'd product after product, went to Vendor-Sponsored "Managed Services Sales Trainings" on their Tools, and really put forth our best Sales effort. I'm serious - Really.

Guess what? We finally concluded that, while there may be companies out there selling Network Monitoring (as Managed Services) as a Stand-Alone product, and being tremendously successful at it, we simply were not one of them.

Does that seem as ironic to you as it does to us? I mean, we've got the egos that come with being a Technically-Proficient, Successful IT Company, for Pete's sake! We think we're pretty darn good Marketers and Sales People, too - **LOL**!

So why did we fail?

All I can tell you is that we've spoken with lots of other IT Partners that tried - just like we did - to sell Network Monitoring as a standalone service, and *who were successfully able to duplicate our results*. Pretty disappointing, right? So what did we do?

We finally came to the conclusion that we were failing because we could not effectively convey the tremendous value of Proactive Network Monitoring to our Clients. They just could not get past the fact that their networks seemed to be running fine, and if a problem did crop up, *we were right there to take care of it for them*. Wonderful.

We were so good at what we did, our Clients were supremely confident that we could continue to take care of any eventuality. Don't misinterpret me, it's great to have such a trusting relationship with our Clients, but in this situation it was actually hurting us! We had inadvertently become our own worst enemy by being so effective. Some of our Clients wanted things just the way they were – and that meant they wanted us to remain Reactive!

How do you demonstrate the value of something that's basically unquantifiable before it's implemented?

The good news is, we did finally figure it out, and adjusted our model accordingly. Once we understood that the problem wasn't with the service, but with the Client's perception of the Service, we were able to get to work.

We decided that the best way to sell Proactive Network Monitoring was not as a Lead Product or Service. Heck, we decided not to sell it at all! We rolled it into our Managed Services offering *as an additional benefit.*

Since we couldn't convey to our Clients how much of a benefit Network Monitoring is to us, and in turn, to them, we went about it a completely different way - *we bundled it.*

So now our Clients receive the benefit of Proactive Network Monitoring, as well as Unlimited Remote Help Desk Support *and* Vendor Management. A Triple Play! Everybody wins.

And almost everybody gets it...

Pricing Managed Services

People want economy and they will pay any price to get it.

Lee Iacocca (1924 -)

There are numerous ways to price Managed Services Offerings, and it's ultimately up to you to choose the pricing model that makes the most sense for you. The following are just a few of the pricing models we've seen implemented, and the Managed Services Partners and Providers that we've worked with have all experienced varying degrees of success with each one:

The "All-You-Can Eat", Flat-Fee Pricing Model

This is our personal favorite, and the model that we promote and train our Managed Services Partners in. This model tremendously benefits the Managed Services Provider as well as the Client. For the Provider, it allows the freedom to customize the Monthly Fee in each and every Service Agreement for maximum profitability. With our methodology, during the Sales process, we illustrate how much money the Client loses each and every month that they <u>do not</u> enlist our Services.

We have found this to be an extremely effective method of closing a sale, as opposed to any of the other Pricing Models we're about to discuss.

Because our Sales Presentation is based upon how much we can potentially <u>save</u> the Client when they enlist our Services, we have consistently been able to sign Clients to Agreements worth much more than other pricing models might allow. There are several variations to this model, but the general concept is to provide a Flat-Fee for all Support rendered to the Client each month, and can include Remote Support, Onsite Support, Lab/Bench time, or all three.

This model is extremely flexible, and may include providing Flat-Fee Services during certain hours and/or days of the month only, with additional charges billed for Services rendered outside of those times. Or the Flat Fee may cover only Remote Support, with Onsite Visits and Lab or Bench Time billable separately, or any combination of these. The primary goal is to provide the Client the ability to realistically budget their IT Support costs over a year's time, and experience no extraordinary billing fluctuations.

This is a radically different Sales Technique than the Prospective Client has probably ever seen before from an IT Company, and because it is so different than what they are accustomed to, or expect – it's tremendously successful.

We illustrate exactly how we execute this successful Managed Services Sales Technique later on in this book, and exactly how we use the *Existing Client Cost Analysis*[*] for existing Clients and the *New Client Savings Analysis*[*] for New Clients to accomplish it.

---

[*] *Included as a download*

The "Per Device" Pricing Model

This pricing model is fairly simple, and many Managed Services Providers utilize it primarily for its simplicity. The premise is to develop a Flat Fee for each type of Device that is supported in a Client's environment. For instance, a basic Per Device pricing model might designate a Flat Fee of $49 per Desktop, $199 per Server, $29 per Network Printer and $99 per Network managed.

The benefits of this Pricing Model are the fact that it is very easy to quote and illustrate costs for Prospective Clients, as well as the facility it affords the SMB IT Service Provider to modify the Monthly Service Fee as the Client adds additional devices in the future.

Something to think about when evaluating this model is that it can lend itself to selling Managed Services based more upon Price, rather than Benefit. The experienced SMB IT Service Provider will realize this, and will modify their Sales Presentation accordingly.

The "Gold/Silver/Bronze" Pricing Model

This model may be the most popular among Managed Services Providers we've spoken with. The premise is to build several bundled packages of Services, with each increasingly more expensive package providing more Services to the Potential Client.

For instance, a "Bronze" Desktop Managed Services package may include basic phone and remote support, Patch Management and Virus and AdWare Removal for an entry-level price. Bumping up to the higher-priced "Silver" Desktop Managed Services package may include Onsite Visits, and the "Gold" package may include Emergency After-Hours Support, being the highest-priced package. This Pricing Model lends itself well to all devices in the Client's environment.

Additional Services to round out a full offering with the "Bronze, Silver, Gold" Pricing Model are usually made available á la carte.

The "Pick 5" Pricing Model

This Managed Services Pricing Model is an interesting combination of the "Gold, Silver, Bronze" Pricing Model with an "á la carte" twist. The basic premise here is to identify three or more successively higher-priced categories with a list of Services available in each. The Client gets his choice of picking a set number of Services from the one Category they wish their Managed Services Agreement to cover.

For instance, let's say we have Categories named Basic, Advanced and Premium. In the Basic category we have 8 Services available to choose from, including Phone Support, Remote Support, Patch Management, AdWare Management, License Management, Case Management, Backup Management and Monitoring. The Client would choose 5 of these, and a Service Agreement would be created to support them.

For the Advanced Category, we might add Limited After-Hours and Onsite Support for a higher Flat Fee than the Basic Category, allowing the Client to choose from these additional Services.

The Premium Category may include Emergency 24 Hour Support, 1 Hour Response Time and Disaster Recovery of the Server(s) as additional options; for a higher Flat Fee than the Basic and Advanced Categories, and the Client would now be able to choose from these additional Services to create their Managed Services Support Plan.

SMB IT Service Providers contemplating the implementation of this Pricing Model should carefully choose the minimum required Services available in each Category, to insure that they are selected, in order to provide the best possible Proactive Support for the Client.

The "Á La Carte" Pricing Model

Possibly the most difficult Pricing Model to sell and maintain, the "Á La Carte" model may be the least popular discussed in this section. The basic premise of this Pricing Model is to allow the Client to pick and choose the Managed Services they would like, from a large menu of individually priced Services.

The dangers inherent with a Pricing Model of this type include giving the Client too many decisions to make, thereby slowing the sale. The more choices the Client needs to make, the more confused they might get, leading them to skip selecting Services that they really need, and/or choosing Services that might not be so critical to their particular environment.

In addition, this Pricing Model may again skew the Client's perception of these Services to a cost, rather than a benefit perspective. To top it all off, putting together the Managed Services Agreement for the "Á La Carte" Pricing Model is the most time-consuming of all models in this discussion.

The "Monitoring Only" Pricing Model

Normally only seen in Medium to Enterprise engagements, usually where the Client has In-House IT Staff, the "Monitoring Only" Pricing Model provides Network Monitoring Services and Alerting to the SMB IT Service Provider, the Client's In-House IT Staff, or both.

In this scenario, several different Service Levels can be employed, from a very basic requirement to forward all Alerts to the Client's In-House IT Staff only, allowing them to address and perform all Incident Resolution, to a scenario where the SMB IT Service Provider participates in basic Incident Resolution or even more advanced Support.

The SMB IT Service Provider may also simply resell their chosen Vendor's Network Monitoring Service to the Client in a larger environment, and have no direct or indirect responsibility after the sale.

We believe that whichever Managed Services Pricing Model you choose, you should always have a "Monitoring Only" Service available to market to your Clients.

As mentioned in the beginning of this chapter, the Managed Services Pricing Model you ultimately select is completely up to you, and will depend on many factors, including:

- Your current Pricing Model and the ease of transitioning it

- The size and competency of your Staff

- The number of Clients you currently serve and the size and complexity of their environments

- The Managed Services Monitoring Tools and Practice Management Software you will be utilizing

- How difficult your Clients will be to transition.

Selling Managed Services to Existing Clients

The jungle is dark but full of diamonds...

Arthur Miller (1915 - 2005), *Death of a Salesman*

Now that we've gotten past everything that needed to be digested before we could discuss selling Managed Services, we can discuss selling Managed Services!

How exactly do we sell Managed Services? Well, that's the most important question that we need to answer, isn't it? I mean, it's obvious to many of us that Managed Services offer real, quantifiable value to our Clients (and ourselves), but if we can't sell it, nothing else really matters, does it?

Now, there are two different sales scenarios you'll find yourself in. The first is selling Managed Services to your existing Clients. The second is selling Managed Services to new Clients.

I will submit to you that in many cases, selling Managed Services to your existing Clients will prove more difficult than selling to new Clients. Why is that? Well, there are several reasons. Remember the example earlier, where our Clients did not immediately grasp the value of Proactive Network Monitoring, because we had done such a splendid job of maintaining their networks in the past? You will encounter a similar reaction from your existing Clients regarding Managed Services.

Think about this –

Your biggest obstacle in transitioning to this new model is your image.

What has your Client's perception been of your company thus far? If you've done a good job of marketing yourself and conducting business as a Trusted Advisor and true Solution Provider, then your task will be made easier.

If; however, you've operated in "break-fix" mode, and your Client perceives you as a Reactive resource, it will be more challenging for you to change that perception.

But that's exactly what needs to occur, if you're to succeed in transitioning your existing "A" Clients to the Managed Services model.

Did you notice that I said "A" Clients? That was intentional – remember the statement earlier about the "C" Clients robbing you of the time you should be spending with your "A" Clients? Guess what – no matter what your business model is, "break-fix" or Managed Services, *your "C" Clients will still be "C" Clients*. Plus, it's more difficult to change a "C" Client's perception than it is an "A" Client's.

That's not to say; however, that the occasional "C" Client won't surprise you. We've had "C" Clients that we never thought would "get it" and move to Managed Services, but guess what? With the proper presentation, they did! So we ended up with a few "C" Clients that made the transition, and eventually became "A" Clients after a while. I guess that just proves that you can't ever count anyone out – *even though these were definitely our exceptions to the rule*.

I'm sure you've noticed by now that we haven't addressed "B" Clients at all. *That's because "B" Clients can go either way.* What I mean is this - you have "B" Clients that can be converted to "A" Clients with the right effort and attention. But the opposite is also true – *you may have "B" Clients that are really "C" Clients in disguise.* And I'll bet you know exactly who they are, too. So we'll leave the "B" Clients to you to decide how you'd like to handle them moving forward.

Image

A rock pile ceases to be a rock pile the moment a single man contemplates it, bearing within him the image of a cathedral.

Antoine De Saint-Exupery (1900 - 1944)

The most important and most difficult process that you will need to undergo when transitioning to the Managed Services model is reinventing yourself and your company's image. This is especially true for your existing Clients. As we discussed earlier, you are defined primarily by the manner in which you've provided services to your Clients in the past. If you've provided "break-fix" services, then you will be perceived as a Reactive "break-fix" company. If you've provided Solutions, and have dealt with your Clients primarily on that level, then you will be defined as a Solution Provider and Trusted Advisor.

Just remember this – it doesn't matter at all how *you perceive* your services and how *you feel* they've been delivered to your Clients. What counts is *how they perceive your services*. I'm sure you've heard the phrase "perception is reality". This is certainly never truer than in the IT industry.

So let's take this essential process and break it down for your two Client groups – existing Clients, then new Clients. Let's take existing Clients first.

As mentioned, we'll need to change, or at least modify this group's perception of your company and its service model. What we basically want to do is pound our chests and shout from the highest mountaintop "WE'RE NO LONGER A BREAK-FIX COMPANY!" While that might feel great, it won't do much towards achieving our re-imaging goal!

What we're actually going to do is very close to the mountaintop exercise. But instead of climbing Everest and shouting to the world (while gasping in the thin air, where sound doesn't travel very far), we're going to convey the same message via a small Marketing Campaign.

Before we continue; however, let's take a moment and discuss the importance of changing your own internal perception of your image. I'm sure you've noticed that throughout this book, we've used the word "Client" exclusively, instead of "Customer". This is intentional – as a Trusted Advisor, we have Clients, much the same as an Attorney or CPA does.

This term denotes an active, longstanding <u>Relationship</u>, whereas the term "Customer" more closely signifies a person who purchases a commodity, like a Convenience Store patron that pulls in to buy a soft drink. You see – *you also need to change your internal image of yourself* as well, if you want to change your Client's external perception of your image. You need to believe you are, and *begin acting the role of* the Trusted Advisor. This Inner Perception will modify your own Outward Reality.

Okay – back to the Marketing Campaign!

The Marketing Campaign that you will launch to re-image yourself can take many forms, but we're going to cover just three simple, effective actions that you can execute immediately. These are:

1. A letter to your existing Clients

2. A phone call to your existing Clients

3. A Meeting with your existing Clients

Sounds like a pretty basic plan, right? In our experience, this process has been both easy to accomplish, as well as effective. We've included a sample *Managed Services Introduction Letter*[*] with this book to get you started.

You'll need to modify our sample letter to fit on your letterhead and create a mail merge with your existing Clients' contact information, sign the letters and send them out.

Wait a few days, and then follow up on each and every letter with a personal phone call. *Don't sell Managed Services on the phone.* You're just setting an appointment to come out and spend 15 minutes with your Client. Let them know that you have a short presentation that you need to present to them in person, and that it can't be done over the phone.

---

[*] *Included as a download*

The day before the appointment, call again and confirm. If you receive any objections, simply re-state that you only need 15 minutes. *Just make sure you set the appointment.*

Familiarize yourself with the *Managed Services Client PowerPoint Presentation*[*]. You can either print the eight slides in the deck out *IN COLOR*, or run the presentation from your laptop during the meeting. The choice is up to you.

DO NOT EMAIL THE PRESENTATION TO YOUR CLIENT AHEAD OF TIME.

---

[*] *Included as a download*

First Client Meeting

Change is the process by which the future invades our lives.

Alvin Toffler

Once you've confirmed your first Client meeting, arrive early and prepared to present your new Managed Services model to your Client. The key factor to impress upon your Client is that you are no longer a "break-fix" company, and are transitioning to a Proactive IT Service Delivery model that will provide your Client better support and increased uptime, while saving on costs. Illustrate the 6 benefits we discussed earlier, that your Client will receive as a result of moving to your new Proactive Managed Services model.

It is important that you do not try to close your Client on any Managed Services at this meeting.

You are simply taking the time to explain the new direction your company is moving towards, and letting your Client know how important they are to you. You would like to schedule another meeting to sit down with your Client to perform a Managed Services Cost Analysis, to accurately determine the Flat-Rate monthly fee you will be able to offer your Client through your new Managed Services model. We have included the <u>Managed Services Cost Analysis</u>* with this book for your use *with existing Clients,* and the <u>Managed Services Savings Analysis</u>* for your use *with new Clients.*

In many cases, you will be able to save your Client money, in others you may quote them the same as the average amount they spent with you the previous year, and in a few cases you may actually charge the Client more per month than they are accustomed to paying. This is why it is so important that you follow the *<u>Managed Services Client PowerPoint Presentation</u>*,* as it does a great job of highlighting the benefits of the Managed Services model for your Client.

Remember – the goal is to transition as many of your existing Clients over to the Managed Services model as possible, *even if you have to bill them no more than you did the previous year* (hopefully you'll be able to justify increasing your monthly fees as you'll be performing more Services for your Clients). Why is

---

* *Included as a download*

this so important? Because the more Clients you transition, the less Reactive you'll be, the more your Valuation will increase, and you'll receive all of the other benefits we've discussed previously that delivering Managed Services will afford you.

Once your Client has agreed to schedule your next meeting, *schedule it right then and there*. And try not to reschedule it later (you'll lose momentum and your Client's availability). Thank them for their time, and move on to the next Client. It's important that you visit each and every Client in this manner, in order to qualify and prepare them for your transition. It is equally important that you follow through with the next Managed Services Cost Analysis appointment. Remember – don't lose momentum, it's difficult to gain back.

Tip:

Do not schedule any of these important "transitioning" meetings immediately before, during or after you have, or are scheduled to perform, any Onsite Services for your Clients.

It's important to set the appropriate tone with your Clients during these meetings – Business Owner to Business Owner.

It's difficult to convey the proper tone for these meetings with your Client right after you've crawled out from under a user's (or your Client's) desk!

Once you've successfully met with all of your existing Clients and presented your new Managed Services model to them, you're to be congratulated! You've just taken the most important step towards transitioning to the Managed Services model.

But even though it's the most important step, it's just the beginning.

Transition

Life is pleasant. Death is peaceful. It's the transition that's troublesome.

Isaac Asimov (1920 - 1992)

Okay, you've successfully met with all of your existing Clients and presented them with your new Managed Services model – now what? You've told everybody that you're a Managed Services Provider, so now it's time to get to work.

It's obvious that the cornerstone to your successful Managed Services offering includes Network Monitoring, Remote Help Desk Support and Vendor Management, and you either need to provide these services directly to your Clients yourself, or find a Fulfillment Partner to share some of the heavy lifting.

Let's assume for the moment that you've got that part figured out. How do you then leverage the momentum you've built with your existing Clients, and get them to sign on as Managed Services Clients after your initial meeting?

This is actually a two-step process. The first step is to gather the information you need in order to complete the _Managed Services Cost Analysis_*. The second is to present your findings to your Client, and if it makes sense for them, sign them to a Managed Services Agreement.

You noticed that I used the term "if it makes sense for them", didn't you? Well, let's be clear on this point. _Managed Services simply doesn't make sense for every Client_. There, I've said it – and it needed to be said. There are many reasons why this might be true:

1. Client's account is too small to justify cost vs. benefit

2. Client doesn't "get it"

3. (You fill in the blank)

Remember – you may not be able to transition every single one of your Clients to the Managed Services model, so be mentally prepared for this possibility. Also remember that _this_

---

* _Included as a download_

is a good thing. The Clients that don't fit the model, or don't "get it" need to go away.

Did that last sentence sound a bit harsh? It's not intended to; it's simply stating a fact. If you're to successfully achieve your Exit Strategy, you can't "double-dip". You can't serve two masters – Reactive "break-fix" and Proactive Managed Services Clients. If you're transitioning to Managed Services, *you need to transition completely to Managed Services.*

Why?

Because you need to stop being Reactive, and your old "break-fix" Clients (that don't "get it") *like you just the way you are.* It works great for them – something breaks, and they call you. Of course they need it fixed right away! They don't care if you're in the middle of a dozen other things. They've been your good Client for years, haven't they?

You owe it to them to drop whatever you're doing and deal with their immediate need.

Right now!

Why should they think any differently?

Isn't that what you've always done?

If you're serious about reaching your goal, you're going to have to make some of the toughest decisions you've ever made with your good old, reliable "break-fix" Clients. And it's hard - we know. We went through it too, and believe me; we'd do it again in a heartbeat – and next time with a lot less anxiety!

I think you understand. Your biggest obstacle during transition will be your own _fear of risk_. The dreaded "what if's". "What if none of my Clients "get it"? "What if I lose all of that "break-fix" revenue that's kept me going all this time"? "What if I can't find good Fulfillment Partners to help me"?

How about this:

What if you keep doing exactly what you're doing now?

Will anything change?

Will providing Services to your Clients get any easier?

Will you be able to take time off?

Will you be able to sell your company some day and retire?

Okay, soapbox time is over. By purchasing this book, you've taken the first step towards exploring how to implement effective change in your business through the Managed Services model. From here on out, we'll assume you're serious about transitioning, and will follow the methods we've outlined to achieve transition to a complete Managed Services revenue model. Let's go!

Second Client Meeting

It's not that some people have willpower and some don't. It's that some people are ready to change and others are not.

James Gordon, M.D.

It's already time for your second Client Meeting – wow, that was quick! Before you sit down with your Client, make sure you review the *Managed Services Cost Analysis*[*] form, and understand it completely. This and the *Managed Services Savings Analysis*[*] form are extremely powerful tools, because they actually *dollarize* how much money your Client <u>loses</u> each month by <u>not</u> accepting your Managed Services Agreement.

By following the instructions in the next Chapter for completing the *Managed Services Cost Analysis*[*] form, you will be able to gather all of the information necessary to provide your Client with a cost analysis reflecting what he or she is currently

---

[*] *Included as a download*

paying on a yearly basis to manage their own Vendors, and for Reactive IT support. You'll also be able to reflect what cost savings (if any) they can expect to receive from your Managed Services model.

Okay, it's true – you might not be able to reflect any cost savings to your Client each and every time with this analysis – *that's why we don't sell on cost savings, but on benefit* (faster response time, maximum uptime, Vendor Management, etc.). And in almost every case, we try to bundle-in savings from another Value-Added service (such as an Integrated T1) to help our analysis.

An important note to consider – in some cases, we have actually dropped our Managed Services fees from what our Client's average historical monthly billing had been. It just made sense for us in certain situations, as the cost to support certain Clients dropped significantly. And believe me – there's no better way to get a Client to sign on for Managed Services than to show them they'll actually be paying less for better, Proactive Support!

So now you're sitting in front of your Client, and will conduct their Managed Services Cost Analysis. Simply gather all of the information required to complete this form. This meeting realistically shouldn't take you more than 15 minutes with existing Clients, and it's important that you conduct it in person, and not over the phone. Also, the same rules apply as they did for your first meeting – your sole purpose for this meeting is to conduct the Managed Services Cost Analysis.

DO NOT LEAVE THE COST ANALYSIS BEHIND FOR THE CLIENT TO FILL OUT.

Once this is done, thank your Client, and inform them that you will be compiling the results of your interview and preparing a Managed Services quote for them.

Tip:

It's a good idea to schedule your follow-up appointment with your Client now, rather than risk playing phone-tag with them later.

By following the instructions in the following Chapter for completing the *Managed Services Cost Analysis*[*], you will find out what your Client's Total Existing Annual IT Support Costs are. Let's say this number is $10,000, for example. You will now need to propose a Flat Monthly Managed Services Fee that your Client will agree to.

The best case scenario in this example would be one where you could bill your Client at least $850 per month, as it would be an easy decision for your Client to agree to your Managed Services proposal when you're not increasing what they're currently spending.

Remember – the amount you actually end up quoting your Client per month may actually be more than what they're currently spending on your Services. With the *Managed Services Cost Analysis*[*] tool, you're simply dollarizing the real, hidden costs of your Client dealing (successfully or unsuccessfully) with their Vendors themselves, and the benefits of transferring those costs and responsibilities to you.

---

[*] *Included as a download*

So in this scenario, you're able to provide your Client better Services for (hopefully) no more money than they're used to paying you. They can now open one Trouble Ticket with you for anything that goes wrong in their environment, and focus on running their Business, not their Vendors.

Let's again summarize your Client's Managed Services benefits:

1. Experience Increased Operational Efficiency

2. Control their Operating Costs

3. Cost-effectively gain access to Enterprise-Level Support

4. Experience Minimized Downtime

5. Can now focus on running their Business, not their Vendors

6. Realize peace of mind knowing their Network is being monitored 24/7

And what are your benefits? You're able to bill each of your Managed Services Clients a Flat Fee *in advance* each and every month, perform your services *Proactively*, *Remotely*, and can focus on *Delivering Solutions* to your Clients.

Let's again recap your benefits:

1. Realize the benefits of an Annuity-Based revenue model

2. Enjoy Long-Term, Predictable revenue growth

3. Eliminate the cycles of "*Feast or Famine*"

4. Bill Independently of Any Specific Technician

5. Stop trading time for money

6. Do Much More with Less

7. Eliminate Invoice Haggling

8. Sell Solutions Much More Easily

9. Increase your Company's Valuation

Prepare Your Managed Services Cost Analysis

Collecting the information required, and completing the *Managed Services Cost Analysis for Existing Clients*[*] is very simple.

What we are attempting to do is leverage the cost savings that managing the Client's Vendors will provide them, as well as to again illustrate all of the additional benefits the Client will receive by transitioning to Proactive Managed Services.

We realistically could gather the information required to complete the *Managed Services Cost Analysis for Existing Clients*[*] over the phone, but we strongly recommend taking the time to meet face-to-face with Clients and their Vendor Managers during this transition, as it will help accomplish our objective much more easily. It's no surprise that it's always easier to sell a Client a Product or Service when doing so in person, rather than over the phone. In addition, we're continually looking for opportunities to meet with our Clients in order to strengthen our Relationships.

---

[*] *Included as a download*

So we're basically going to meet with our existing Clients to ask them how many Vendors Service their organization, and find out who in the company deals with all of their Vendor issues, if we don't already know. We'll then request permission from the Client to speak with that person directly.

Let's say the Office Manager deals with all Vendor issues in this example. We will ask for their assistance in gathering important Vendor Data for our records. We always conduct this short interview in a very conversational manner. After we find out who all of the Vendors are, and note them on our *Vendor Management Form*[*], we ask the Office Manager which piece of equipment, 3rd-Party Line-of-Business Application, or Vendor Service they spend the most time troubleshooting.

There will invariably be a problem piece of equipment (such as a Network Copier) or 3rd-Party Line of Business Software Application that they will volunteer, and let you know just how frustrated they have become from having to deal with it.

If we're lucky, the Office Manager will provide us with enough examples like this that it won't be difficult to convince them, or

---

[*] *Included as a download*

our Client, that having us perform Vendor Management is a good idea.

Now that we've let the Office Manager vent a while, we're going to ask them how many hours per week they think they spend, on average, managing all of the Vendors we've listed. Remember – we're going to list each and every Infrastructure or Software Vendor that supports their entire organization:

- Telco Service Vendor

- Telco System Vendor

- Broadband Service Vendor

- Copier Vendor

- Printer Vendor

- Fax Vendor

- Hardware Vendor

- Line-of-Business Application Vendor

- Web Hosting Vendor

- Co-Lo Vendor

- Cellular Vendor

- POS Vendor

- All Other Infrastructure Vendors

We will be using the "Managed Services Existing Client Cost Analysis" downloadable after registering this book at www.mspu.us/bookregistration *for this scenario. Launch or Print it out to follow along...*

Get the idea? Okay, so let's say the Office Manager tells us that there are 12 Vendors that support their environment. We

enter this information on the *Managed Services Cost Analysis**
form under "Number of Vendors Managed by Client".

They then proceed to inform us that they spend about 3 hours
per week (12 hours per month) dealing with all of these
Vendors (we always ask for weekly hours, they always seem
higher than when we ask for monthly hours).

We now enter this information on the *Managed Services Cost
Analysis** form under "Number of Hours Spent Managing
Vendors per Month".

We then find out from our Client what the Office Manager's
Salary is, including bonuses, benefits, sick leave and vacation
time, and calculate what their hourly pay is – DO NOT ASK
THE OFFICE MANAGER FOR THIS INFORMATION.

We then enter this data on the Cost Analysis form as well,
under "Manager's Average Hourly Rate", which will then be
used to calculate how much revenue (not to mention

---

* *Included as a download*

productivity) the Client is losing per year by having the Office Manager perform these duties.

So let's say we've calculated the Office Manager's true hourly rate to be $45.00 per hour. Our Cost Analysis form will reflect a value of $6,480.00 per year ($45.00 per hour X 12 hours per month X 12 Months) as "Revenue Lost Annually to Managing Vendors". Using this formula, we can extrapolate a loss of more than $32,000.00 over a 5 year period for the Client. These are real dollars impacting the Client's bottom line!

We have now gathered all of the Data needed from the Client, and can complete the Analysis back at our offices, where we will determine how much we billed the Client the previous year IN LABOR HOURS ONLY – *no Project Labor or Hardware billing*. We take this number and enter it on the Managed Services Cost Analysis form under "Existing Annual IT Costs".

Let's use $10,000.00 in this example. Once this value is entered on the Cost Analysis, it will automatically be added to the "Annual Loss of Revenue from Client Vendor Manager" value at the bottom of the form, and calculates a "Total Existing Annual IT Support Costs" value of $16,480.00.

We now have all of the information we need in order to quote a value in the "Proposed Managed Services Cost" field on the Analysis. Because of the fact that we will be handling the Vendor Management, as well as providing Unlimited Help Desk Support and Network Monitoring, we will quote this Client at least $17,000.00 per year, or about $1,400.00 per month.

If this Client is one of our "A" Clients, and "gets it", we should have very little resistance in closing this sale. We always propose a higher fee; rather than a lower, or matching fee, from the historical billing we have performed for existing Clients. It's easy to lower our Monthly Fees in order to win business, but difficult - or impossible, to raise them after we realize we could have quoted more…

Prepare Your Managed Services Quote

If you really do put a small value upon yourself, rest assured that the world will not raise your price.

Anonymous

After performing your Managed Services Cost Analysis, you'll know exactly how much your Client is spending on managing their Vendors themselves, as well as on their existing IT Support with you. At this point, you'll be able to determine what you will quote your Client for your Managed Services offering.

This will either be a no-brainer (if you can quote your Client a price that's slightly more, less than, or equal to what they're currently paying), or more challenging, if you can't make the numbers work in order to reflect an acceptable profit. When all else fails, we have a rule of thumb that we use when pricing Managed Services for Existing Clients; which has served us well, and entails the use of the *Profitability Matrix*[*] tool included with this book.

---

[*] *Included as a download*

By using the Profitability Matrix, you can quickly document all of your existing Clients, the number of their Desktops, Servers, Networks and Network Printers, and what you billed them the previous year from a LABOR ONLY perspective - make sure to only enter the Labor billing for normal support the previous year – *no Project Labor or any Hardware billing.*

Now that you've entered all of the physical Labor costs for historical support on the Profitability Matrix, it will calculate what you would bill these existing Clients using the following default flat fees from a Managed Services Perspective:

Default Profitability Matrix Pricing:

Desktops: $69/mo

Printers: $29/mo

Networks: $99/mo

Servers: $299/mo

So, by using this rule of thumb, for a Client with 1 Server, 1 Firewall/Router, 20 Desktops, and 2 Network Printers, your fee would be $1,836 per month or $22,032.00 per year.

As I indicated, this is just a rule of thumb. In many cases, we use this tool to simply get a quick idea of what our minimum fees would be, and then compare that number against what our Managed Services Cost Analysis reflects.

For example, if this same Client were currently spending $2,000 per month, as reflected by our Managed Services Cost Analysis, and we could only win the Client's transition business by lowering their costs, we could successfully propose billing them $1,800 per month for Managed Services, and save them $2,400 per year.

But how can we be sure that this fee isn't too low to support?

In this scenario, we would use the Profitability Matrix to insure that we wouldn't under-quote the Client for Services, and then use the highest monthly billing rate possible to quote a Managed Services Agreement. It's a true Win-Win for all Parties. Better yet, we now have a possible budget of $2,400 to apply towards Solutions!

What we really want to achieve with the Managed Services Profitability Matrix is to come up with a yearly price for each of your Existing Clients that is very close to what you billed them the previous year. We accomplish this by filling out the entire Managed Services Profitability Matrix, and then modifying the default price for Desktops. If your Monthly Managed Services pricing is much higher than what you charged your Clients overall, drop the $69 price per Desktop until pricing comes in-line. If it is less, then increase the Desktop pricing. We normally don't modify the default minimum pricing for any of the other devices in the environment.

Experiment with the Profitability Matrix included as a download available after registering this book at www.mspu.us/bookregistration **until you have a good idea of what your absolute minimum billing should be when transitioning each of your Existing Clients.**

Remember – this is simply an internal exercise for you to determine how to prevent yourself from charging less for each of your Existing Clients' Managed Services Agreements than you should, and not a recommendation on what your actual pricing should be for your Clients. *Consider it your "Stop-Loss" process.*

The Closer:

A sure way to motivate your Clients to sign your Managed Services Agreements is to include Recovery of their Server(s) to their original state before any Disaster. If you're doing your job, you will average so few of these, that they become insignificant in the big picture. Since we've included this clause in all of our Managed Services Agreements, we've signed just about every Client we've approached!

Another good tip is to include ALL Service (Remote, Onsite and Lab/Bench Time) between the hours of 8am and 5pm Monday through Friday in your Flat Monthly Fee. As mentioned earlier, this is also a great psychological selling technique. Because of the fact that we only go Onsite when there is a physical hardware failure or other extraordinary circumstance; like a Vendor Meet (remember, we close almost all Trouble Ticket requests remotely), we're not going Onsite any more times than we would otherwise, so the Clients really appreciate your rolling all Remote, Onsite and Lab/Bench Time Services into their one Flat Fee per month.

Now that you're comfortable with the monthly fee you'll be quoting your Client, you're ready to prepare your Managed

Services Agreement. We've included a *Sample Managed Services Agreement*[*] with this book for your review.

---

[*] *Included as a download*

Prepare Your Managed Services Agreement

As noted previously, we've included a *Sample Managed Services Agreement** with this book for your review.

This Agreement is not meant for you to utilize as-is, it is only included as an example for you to compare with your own Agreements. There is simply no way to develop a Global Agreement that will meet every single SMB IT Provider's needs, nor protect them from a Legal position.

Please have your Legal Team or Attorney review each and every form and document you utilize in your business to make certain that your rights, as well as your Clients', are protected.

There are several items to appreciate when reviewing the enclosed Sample Managed Services Agreement. You will immediately note that the Term of the Agreement is for 3 Years, and automatically renews for a subsequent 3-Year Term. The longer the Term of your Agreements, the higher their (as well as your organization's) overall value.

Included as a download

You will also note that the Termination Clause in this Sample Agreement is for Cause only – meaning that the Client needs to notify you of any perceived material breach of the Agreement on your part, and allow you 30 days to rectify it.

The Agreement also goes into granular detail in regards to Coverage, Support and Escalation, Service outside Normal Working Hours, Service Calls Where No Trouble is found, and Limitation of Liability.

It also details specifically what Services, Equipment and Software Applications are included, as well as what is excluded from Support, and documents the Minimum Standards the environment must meet in order to qualify for Services.

We have also specified Response and Resolution Times, a definition of Support Tiers, and both a written and graphical representation of a Help Desk Escalation Process.

The Sample Managed Services Agreement also documents Flat Monthly Fee pricing, as well as pricing for requested Services which fall outside of Flat-Fee Support.

Once you've put your own Managed Services Agreement together, you're ready to present it to your Client.

Third Client Meeting – Sign 'Em Up!

To follow, without halt, one aim: There's the secret of success.

Anna Pavlova (1885 - 1931)

If you've followed our directions and conducted your previous meetings effectively with your Client, you should have very little resistance in getting them to sign your Managed Services Agreement.

Present your *Managed Services Cost Analysis*[*] findings to your Client, reiterate the benefits they will receive from your new model, and sign them up. We always bring two copies of our Agreements, and countersign the signature page with the Client, after which we each keep a copy for our records.

Something that we always do, and strongly recommend to our Partners, is to *go over the Managed Services Agreement with*

---

[*] *Included as a download*

the Client in detail, reviewing each section carefully. This process may take an extra 20 to 30 minutes during your final Appointment, but it is worth all the time that it takes, as it establishes the correct expectations with the Client regarding your Services, and how they are delivered. It also gives the Client the opportunity to receive clarification on any points they may be unclear on at this point in the process.

This practice has helped us tremendously in building strong relationships with our Clients from the very beginning, and has helped to alleviate misunderstandings later on, after Services have been implemented.

Another task that we make certain to complete once the Agreement has been signed (if we haven't done so already) is to fill out the *Vendor Management Form*[*]. This form documents all of the Client's Infrastructure Vendors, their Contact Information and the Client's Account Information. We use this data when creating the Letters of Agency that we will send out to these Vendors, which establish our Authority over the Client's Vendor relationships.

---

[*] *Included as a download*

Selling Managed Services To New Clients

I can't understand why people are frightened of new ideas.
I'm frightened of the old ones.

John Cage (1912 - 1992)

Selling Managed Services to new Clients will probably be easier for you, especially now that you've had lots of experience transitioning your existing Clients.

One of the reasons that selling to new Clients is easier is that you'll be using our *Managed Services Savings Analysis For New Clients*[*] tool, which allows you to document just how poorly your Prospective Client's network is running, and *dollarizes* how much this Downtime is costing the Client. Let's face it – you're not meeting with a new prospective Client because their network is running fabulously and they're in love with their current IT Provider!

_____

[*] *Included as a download*

In addition to calculating the true cost of Downtime for your prospective new Client, the *Managed Services Savings Analysis** form also documents how much it costs the Client to manage their Vendors themselves, as well as the cost of having their "go-to" In-House Staff Person run around and reboot PC's, perform lightweight troubleshooting, etc., before Management decides to authorize calling in their existing Reactive IT Service Provider to troubleshoot things.

The true magic behind selling to new Clients with the Managed Services Savings Analysis tool is that it conveys to the prospective Client just how much money they lose each and every month <u>they don't</u> sign your Managed Services Agreement!

So our *Managed Services Savings Analysis** form is your best tool when meeting with a new Client. Just follow the directions in the next Chapter on using this form, and proceed with setting up your follow-up appointment. You may also want to schedule a Network Needs Analysis appointment for one of your Engineers or Technicians before or during your second meeting as well. This way you can present the prospective Client a quote to remediate their environment at the same time

---

* *Included as a download*

you present your Managed Services Agreement for signature. You can use the *Needs Analysis*[*] form as a starting point.

The rest of the New Client Sales process follows the steps outlined with selling to your existing Clients. Prepare your Managed Services Agreement, meet with the Client, reiterate the benefits that they will receive by utilizing your Services, and sign them up.

Obviously, the more Clients you sign to a Managed Services Agreement, the more comfortable you'll be, and the easier it will get for you. Set realistic monthly goals for yourself, and you'll quickly see your Exit Strategy becoming a reality.

---

[*] *Included as a download*

Prepare Your Managed Services Savings Analysis

Collecting the information required, and completing the *Managed Services Savings Analysis for New Clients*[*] is very similar to the process utilized with the *Managed Services Cost Analysis for Existing Clients*[*], with a few additional steps.

In addition to leveraging the cost savings that managing the Prospective Client's Vendors will provide them, the *Managed Services Savings Analysis*[*] tool will also reflect the losses the Client incurs by having an In-House Staff Person perform lightweight IT duties before receiving authorization to call in their existing Reactive IT Service Provider.

The Savings Analysis also *dollarizes* what Downtime really costs the Prospective Client, as well as illustrates all of the additional benefits the Client will receive by transitioning to Proactive Managed Services.

Similar to the process we conduct when transitioning an Existing Client to Managed Services, we meet face-to-face with the Prospective Client, their Vendor Manager and their

---

[*] *Included as a download*

designated "Lightweight IT Staff Person" to collect the information we need in order to complete the *Managed Services Savings Analysis*[*] for New Clients.

By "Lightweight IT Staff Person" we're talking about someone in the Prospective Client's organization whose primary job responsibility is anything other than IT, and who has assumed, or inherited, the task of rebooting PC's and performing lightweight troubleshooting to try to "keep things running", before issues escalate to the point that an Onsite visit from the Client's existing, Reactive IT Service Provider is necessary.

Just as with an existing Client, we're going to meet with our Prospective Client to ask them how many Vendors Service their organization, and find out whom in the company deals with all of their Vendor issues. We'll then request permission from the Prospective Client to speak with that person directly.

Let's use the same example here that we did in our Existing Client scenario, and assume that the Office Manager deals with all Vendor issues. We will ask their assistance in

---

[*] *Included as a download*

gathering important Vendor Data in order to prepare our Service Proposal for the Prospective Client.

After we find out who all of the Vendors are, and note them on our *Vendor Management Form*[*], we ask the Office Manager which piece of equipment, 3rd-Party Line-of-Business Application, or Vendor Service they spend the most time troubleshooting, just like we do for Existing Clients.

Again, there will invariably be a problem piece of equipment (such as a Network Copier) or 3rd-Party Line of Business Software Application that they will volunteer, and let you know just how frustrated they are from having to deal with it.

Hopefully, the Office Manager will provide us with enough examples like this that it again won't be difficult to illustrate for them, or the Prospective Client, the value of our Vendor Management Service.

Now that we've let the Office Manager vent a while, we're going to ask them how many hours per week they think is spent, on average, managing all of the Vendors we've listed.

---

[*] *Included as a download*

Remember – we're going to list each and every Infrastructure or Software Vendor that supports the entire organization:

- Telco Service Vendor

- Telco System Vendor

- Broadband Service Vendor

- Copier Vendor

- Printer Vendor

- Fax Vendor

- Hardware Vendor

- Line-of-Business Application Vendor

- Web Hosting Vendor

- Co-Lo Vendor

- Cellular Vendor

- POS Vendor

- All Other Infrastructure Vendors

We will be using the "Managed Services New Client Savings Analysis – Example" form downloadable after registering this book at www.mspu.us/bookregistration *for this scenario. Launch or Print it out to follow along…*

Okay, so let's say the Office Manager tells us there are 12 Vendors. We enter this information on the Managed Services Savings Analysis form under "Number of Vendors Managed by Client".

They then inform us that they spend about 3 hours per week (12 hours per month) dealing with all of these Vendors (we always ask for weekly hours - again, they always seem higher than when we ask for monthly hours).

We now enter this information on the Managed Services Savings Analysis form under "Number of Hours Spent Managing Vendors per Month".

We then find out from our Client what the Office Manager's Salary is, including bonuses, benefits, sick leave and vacation time, and calculate what their pay is hourly – DO NOT ASK THE OFFICE MANAGER FOR THIS INFORMATION.

We enter this data on the Savings Analysis form as well, under "Manager's Average Hourly Rate", which will then be used to calculate how much revenue (not to mention productivity) the Client is losing per year by having the Office Manager perform these duties.

As in our previous example, let's say we've calculated the Office Manager's true hourly rate to be $45.00 per hour. Our *Managed Services Savings Analysis*[*] form will reflect a value of $6,480.00 per year ($45.00 per hour X 12 hours per month X 12 Months) as "Revenue Lost Annually to Managing Vendors". Using this formula, we can extrapolate a loss of

---

[*] *Included as a download*

more than $32,000.00 over a 5 year period for the Client. These are real dollars impacting the Client's bottom line!

We are now going to identify the "Lightweight IT Staff Person". For this example, let's use the Warehouse Manager. We conduct the same type of interview with the Warehouse Manager that we did with the Office Manager.

First we'll ask the Warehouse Manager which PC's are the most problematic in the environment. They will normally promptly identify them for you, and with a little coaxing, proceed to vent to you how much time performing these additional "IT" duties is robbing from their productivity.

It's a simple task, at this point, to ask how many hours a week the Warehouse Manager spends performing these additional tasks. Let's say the Warehouse Manager tells us they spend 3 hours per week (12 hours per month) "keeping things running".

We now enter this information on the Managed Services Savings Analysis form under "Number of Hours Spent Performing IT Functions per Month".

We then find out from our Client what the Warehouse Manager's Salary is, including bonuses, benefits, sick leave and vacation time, and calculate what their pay is hourly – DO NOT ASK THE WAREHOUSE MANAGER FOR THIS INFORMATION.

We then enter this data on the Savings Analysis form as well, under "Staff Member's Average Hourly Rate", which will then be used to calculate how much revenue (not to mention productivity) the Client is losing per year by having the Warehouse Manager perform these duties.

So let's say we've calculated the Warehouse Manager's true hourly rate to be $35.00 per hour. Our Managed Services Savings Analysis form will reflect a value of $5,040.00 per year ($35.00 per hour X 12 hours per month X 12 Months) as "Revenue Lost Annually to Performing IT Functions". Using this formula, we can extrapolate a loss of more than $25,000.00 over a 5 year period for the Client. Once again - these are real dollars impacting the Client's bottom line!

Next, we're going to find out how many Users and Servers exist in the Prospective Client's environment, and enter this data in the appropriate fields on the Savings Analysis form. In this example, let's say there are 20 Users and 1 Server in the environment

Now we're going to find out how many hours of Downtime the environment experiences in regards to Email, Broadband Connectivity, Servers and Desktops. We enter this information in the appropriate fields on the Savings Analysis form as well, which will calculate a Yearly Value for Network Downtime.

So let's assume we've been told that the Client experiences about an hour of Downtime per week for Email and the same for the Broadband Connection, and about an hour every other week that the Server is down for one reason or another.

This adds up to about 10 hours per month, and is reflected on the Savings Analysis as 120 hours per year - good thing you're on the scene! Okay, now we're going to ask the Client what their average Salary is per Employee. Let's say this is $30,000 – this value goes in the "Average Salary per Employee" Field. The Savings Analysis now calculates this value against the amount of Users, and reflects a "Total Employee Yearly Payroll" of $600,000.00. The Savings Analysis tool now calculates "Average Annual Employee Hours", "Total Annual Employee Hours", and "Average Hourly Labor Cost per

Employee". In this example, the average Hourly Labor Cost per Employee is $14.42.

The Savings Analysis now takes $14.42 and multiplies it by 20 Users, and then again by 120 hours of Downtime, for a total Yearly Downtime Cost of $34,615.38.

We're now going to ask the Prospective Client how much they spent on their existing Reactive IT Provider last year - $10,000.00, and enter that value in the "Existing Annual IT Costs" field.

The Managed Services New Client Savings Analysis tool now brings all of the following values down to the bottom of the form:

Annual Loss of Revenue from Client Vendor Manager

$6,480.00

Annual Loss of Revenue from Staff Performing IT Functions

$5,040.00

Annual Loss of Labor Cost from Network Downtime

$34,615.00

Total Existing Annual IT Cost

$10,000.00

The Savings Analysis now totals all of these values and displays:

Total Existing Annual IT Support Costs

$56,135.38

Let's take a moment to fully comprehend and appreciate the awesome power behind this Sales Technique...

I'll guarantee to you that most Prospective Clients have never seen this type of Sales approach from an IT Company before. They are used to having "break-fix" companies come in, count up the equipment, and provide a quote to support it. When a Prospective Client is dealt with in that manner, they can't help but perceive this type of quote as an *expense* – and rightly so. And expenses always negatively impact the bottom line – right?

So what we accomplish with our Managed Services Savings Analysis approach is to differentiate ourselves from any other "break-fix" IT Provider the Client has ever dealt with in the past. We *begin* the Client Relationship from a 50,000 foot "Trusted Advisor" level, setting the appropriate tone and expectation with the Prospective Client right from the initial meeting.

As the Prospective Client realizes that we are looking after *their Bottom Line* – and how we can help to improve it, they are extremely motivated to enlist our Services, as we have performed an excellent job of illustrating how much money they are losing each and every month that they *do not* sign our Managed Services Agreement.

Okay – back to our example.

We've now gathered all of the information we need in order to quote a value in the "Proposed Managed Services Cost" field on the Savings Analysis. And we would argue that you could quote any value in this field up to and including $56,135.38 and be completely confident with that number!

However, we are only going to quote $36,000.00, or $3,000.00 per month, for this Prospective Client. When this value is entered into the "Proposed Managed Services Cost" field on the Analysis, it will reflect a "Total Client Savings" of $20,135.38, or over $1,700.00 per month!

Why would we quote only $3,000.00 per month, if we could quote $4,000.00 per month, and have an excellent chance of getting it? Well, because we noted during our initial Needs Analysis that the Prospective Client really needs to replace their aging Server, as well as 5 PC's with new Desktops.

So what we're going to do is prepare a quote to perform these Infrastructure Upgrades, and present it at the same time we present our Managed Services Agreement for signature. We use this technique to illustrate to our Prospective Client that not only will they benefit from increased uptime, and receive unlimited Help Desk Support as well as Vendor Management

Services, but they will also receive an Infrastructure Upgrade as well – and *it will all still cost less than what they are spending right now!*

When utilized properly, the Managed Services Savings Analysis approach will help you win business over all of the other "break-fix" Proposals you may compete against!

What To Do After Your Client Is Sold

The only place where success comes before work is in the dictionary.

Vidal Sassoon

Wow. Think about this for a minute, and savor it – you've sold your Client on a Managed Services Agreement! I'll bet that just being able to say that has eliminated any doubts that you might have had about being able to sell Managed Services! Congratulations – *but now what?*

Now we do several things:

1. Send the Client a Welcome Letter and Email

2. Bring the Client's Infrastructure up to Minimum Support Levels

3. Create and Mail the Letter of Agency to each of your Client's Vendors

4. Set the Client up in your Help Desk and Monitoring Systems

5. Begin providing Managed Services!

The first thing we'll do is customize the *Managed Services Welcome Letter** and *Managed Services Welcome Email Template** (if you haven't done so already) to welcome your Client to your Managed Services and reiterate your responsibilities under their new Agreement, as well as inform them on how your Help Desk process works, and the ways that they can contact you to request Support.

Secondly, remember our minimum requirements for a Client's Infrastructure in order for them to qualify for our Managed Services?

- All Servers with Microsoft Operating Systems must be running Windows Server 2003 or SBS2003 or later, and have all of the latest Microsoft Service Packs and Critical Updates installed. Non-Microsoft Servers must meet similar OS-Specific requirements.

---

* *Included as a download*

- All Desktop PC's and Notebooks/Laptops with Microsoft Operating Systems must be running Windows XP Pro or later, and have all of the latest Microsoft Service Packs and Critical Updates installed. All Non-Microsoft PC's and Notebooks/Laptops must meet similar OS-Specific requirements.

- All Server and Desktop Software must be Genuine, Licensed and Vendor-Supported.

- The environment must have a currently licensed, up-to-date and Vendor-Supported Server-based Antivirus Solution protecting all Servers, Desktops, Notebooks/Laptops, and Email.

- The environment must have a currently licensed, up-to-date and Vendor-Supported Anti-Spam Solution.

- The environment must have a currently licensed, Vendor-Supported Server or Network-based Backup Solution.

- The environment must have a currently licensed, Vendor-Supported Firewall between the Internal Network and the Internet.

- Any Wireless data traffic in the environment must be securely encrypted.

- The environment must have a T1 or other form of High-Speed Internet Access with Static IP's.

- The environment must contain Spare PC(s)

If your Client's environment is any different than this, you should have previously prepared a quote to bring it up to these minimum standards, and delivered it for approval at the same time that you presented your Managed Services Agreement for signature. Once these standards are met, you can begin providing Monitoring, Help Desk and Vendor Management Services.

Thirdly, print the *Managed Services Letter of Agency*[*] on your Client's Letterhead – one for each of their Vendors. Have your Client sign each one, make copies for your records and send one to each Vendor. It's a good idea to follow up with a phone call to introduce yourself, and reinforce the content of each Letter of Agency.

---

[*] *Included as a download*

The key to Vendor Management is to always maintain your Relationship and the *Primary Position* with your Client. If you can maintain this relationship well, you will be able to anticipate your Client's needs, and recommend Solutions to meet those needs. If these Solutions involve the Client's Vendors, then you will be working with, directing and scheduling them - not only during their normal Support activities, but also throughout the design and implementation of their Solutions.

If the Vendor wishes to present new Solutions to your Client, they will be presenting them to you first, allowing you to decide whether they are good Solutions and will benefit (or even integrate into) the Client's environment.

And the best part?

This process will not be Reactive in any way – but rather, Proactive. You will be in charge, and will be able to minimize mistakes and downtime.

Remember – Vendor Management is also the process through which we identify the great Vendors that "get it" – those that see your position as beneficial to them. Think about it this way: – if a Vendor has a great Solution for a particular Client, wouldn't you champion that Vendor's Solution to the Client, and help the Vendor sell it as the Client's Trusted Advisor? Of course you would!

And if it's good for one Client – wouldn't it be good for others? A good Vendor will see this opportunity immediately. These are the Vendors you would like to add to your Preferred Vendor list – especially after you have worked out some sort of Annuity-Based commission structure with them. *Just like Clients, the "Right" Vendors will get it.*

Also keep in mind that this process will uncover the not-so-great Vendors – those that don't "get it". These Vendors may also not be providing the best Service and Support to the Client, and will soon end up on your list to replace with one of your Preferred Vendors.

When developing relationships with Preferred Vendors, these are just a few of the traits that we look for (many are obvious):

- The Vendor's Customer Service and Support Philosophy must equal our own

- The Vendor must be Technically Proficient and know their product well enough to understand not only what it can do, but also what it can't

- The Vendor must have the ability to provide references for their Product or Solution for Clients in <u>the same</u> Vertical, Type of Business, or environment that our Client is in – we've seen Vendors implement Solutions flawlessly for one particular Client environment, *that failed miserably in a different Client environment*

- The Vendor must have excellent Support for their Product or Service – and during the times of our organization's normal operations

- The Vendor must be willing to work with us through our LOA

- The Vendor must have an Annuity-Based Reseller Compensation Plan that allows their pricing to remain competitive with other similar solutions, and does not penalize the Client through our Reseller relationship

Ultimately, the Vendor we choose for a given Client Solution has to be the best choice for the Client, whether or not we currently have a Partnering relationship with them. And when we don't, we try to establish one as quickly as possible.

Marketing Managed Services - 12 Steps to Success

Success is more a function of consistent common sense than it is of genius.

An Wang

Sales and Marketing.

Sales and Marketing.

Sales and Marketing.

If you're like a lot of SMB IT Service Providers, this term and what it embodies is your *Achilles Heel*, the *Chink in your Armor*, your *Kryptonite*.

Why are so many SMB IT Service Providers challenged in this area? The answer is actually pretty simple – they have not been trained!

Think about all of the time these SMB IT Service Providers spend in Trainings, Webinars, Classes and Self-Study for *Technical Proficiency*. This time could literally amount to hundreds of hours over the years. Now throw in the time spent working Hands-On with Products and Technology, and the number easily *exceeds thousands of hours*!

You can see the analogy I'm building here, right? Just how much time do most SMB IT Service Providers spend in training for Sales and Marketing?

From our experience working with Partners all across the United States - <u>NOT SO MUCH</u>.

I mean, compared to the Technical Hours spent in training and Hands-On time, the time these Providers spend on Sales and Marketing training is virtually:

Nil

Nada

Zilch

Now, of course there are exceptions to every rule – and they know who they are. I'm speaking here to those of you that see my point in themselves – and it's nothing to be ashamed of, it just needs to be identified so that we can address it.

Notwithstanding their lack of Sales and Marketing training, many SMB IT Service Providers do mount successful, consistent Marketing Campaigns and sell new and existing Clients their Products and Services each and every month.

And many don't.

Many SMB IT Service Providers have a Sales Person or Sales Staff to help Market their Products and Services consistently.

And many don't.

Having a well developed, focused Sales and Marketing Process is crucial to being able to forecast revenue beyond 60 or 90 days. It also helps identify target Markets or Verticals, and allows the ability to break away from the inconsistent, reactive Word-of-Mouth Referral technique many SMB IT Service Providers have built their Practices on. A consistent, effective Sales and Marketing Process, simply put, is the key to real growth.

Before working with us, many SMB IT Service Providers offer varying reasons as to why they had not developed a consistent Sales and Marketing Process, and instead relied solely on Word-of-Mouth advertising. Here are a few:

- They were simply too busy to maintain a consistent Sales and Marketing Process

- They had bad experiences Hiring/Training/Managing Sales Staff in the past

- They had planned to implement Sales and Marketing Programs before, or had even spent money on Sales

Systems and Coaching Programs, but were less than successful

- They just didn't know where to start

If you can relate to anything described in this chapter so far, please understand that there is no "miracle" answer to any of these very real challenges. There is absolutely no substitute for training and experience – in any endeavor. But the reality remains that the SMB IT Service Provider *can* learn Technical processes and execute them successfully - and consistently. Otherwise, they would not be in business. This means that we can illustrate a simple, consistent Sales and Marketing Process that they can also learn and execute as well.

Before we get started, let's set the proper expectation – this is a Simple Marketing Process that can be duplicated on a consistent basis to set appointments to present your Services. It is not a full-blown, complex, customized Marketing Program that takes a large Sales Staff to develop and execute. The key to this Process is CONSISTENCY. If you don't have the time to commit to a repeatable process several times a week to grow your business, or can't afford to hire someone on a Part-

Time basis to execute it, *please lower your expectations accordingly.*

Okay, so let's now talk about a simple, repeatable 12-step process that will significantly increase your Managed Services Marketing Success Rate. We have included everything you'll need to accomplish this process as a download available after registering this book at www.mspu.us/bookregistration.

You will be utilizing the following included collateral to accomplish your 12-Step Managed Services Marketing Process:

- Managed Services Marketing Letter or

- Managed Services Marketing Letter to Existing Clients

- Managed Services Introductory Email Template or

- Managed Services Introductory Email Template to Existing Clients

- Managed Services Appointment Confirmation Postcard

- Managed Services Appointment Confirmation Email Template

- Managed Services Client PowerPoint Presentation

- Managed Services Thank-You Postcard

- Managed Services Thank-You Email Template

- Managed Services Cost Analysis for Existing Clients or

- Managed Services Savings Analysis for New Clients

- Managed Services Sample Agreement

Let's walk through each of the 12 Steps for an *existing Client.* The first thing you'll do is modify the *Managed Services Marketing Letter to Existing Cients* * to Mail Merge their Contact Information and print it on your Letterhead. You'll also use the same address list to Mail Merge Envelopes and Labels for Postcards later, so save each list.

------

* Included as a download

Mail these letters out, and wait a few days to make certain your Clients have received them. If you haven't already done so, you'll now modify the appropriate *Managed Services Introductory Email Template*[*] to include your Company information and Logo, and Email it to the same list you've sent your letters to.

These 2 simple actions, when accomplished within days of each other, start to build the foundation on which you will begin to change your image to a Managed Services Provider in your Clients' perception.

The day after you've sent your Email Template, follow up on each and every one with a personal phone call. *Don't sell Managed Services over the phone.* You're just setting an appointment to come out and spend 15 minutes with your Client. Let them know that you have a short presentation that you need to present to them in person, and that it can't be done over the phone.

As soon as the appointment is set, if you haven't already done so, modify the *Appointment Confirmation Email Template*[*] to

---

[*] *Included as a download*

include your Company information and Logo, fill in the appropriate fields, and send it to your Client.

Now if you haven't already done so, also modify the *Appointment Confirmation Postcard Template** to include your Company information and Logo, fill in the appropriate fields, and drop it in the mail.

As you can see, you are continuing to build on the foundation you've created to change your Image by E-Mailing and Mailing this professional collateral to your Client in a consistent and timely manner.

The day before the appointment, call again and confirm. If you receive any objections, simply re-state that you only need 15 minutes. *Just make sure you set the appointment.*

Once you've confirmed the meeting, arrive early and prepared to present your new Managed Services model to your Client.

---

* *Included as a download*

The key factor to impress upon your Client during this meeting is that you are no longer a "break-fix" company, and are transitioning to a Proactive Managed IT Services model that will provide your Client better support and increased uptime, while saving on costs.

It is important that you do not try to close your Client on any Managed Services at this meeting.

You are simply taking the time to explain the new direction your company is moving towards, and letting your Client know how important they are to you. You would like to schedule another meeting to sit down with your Client to perform a Managed Services Cost Analysis, to accurately determine the Flat-Rate monthly fee you will be able to offer your Client through your new Managed Services model. We have included the *Managed Services Cost Analysis*[*] with this book for your use *with existing Clients,* as well as the *Managed Services Savings Analysis*[*] for your use *with new Clients.*

In many cases, you will be able to save your Client money, in others you may quote them the same as the average amount

---

[*] *Included as a download*

they spent with you the previous year, and in a few cases you may actually charge the Client more per month than they are accustomed to paying. This is why it is so important that you follow the *Managed Services Client Presentation PowerPoint Presentation** (after you have modified it to include your Company information and Logo), as it does a great job of highlighting the benefits of the Managed Services model for your Client.

Once your Client has agreed to schedule your next meeting, *schedule it right then and there*. And try not to reschedule it later (you'll lose momentum and your Client's interest). Thank them for their time, and move on to the next Client. It's important that you visit each and every Client in this manner, in order to qualify and prepare them for their transition. It is equally important that you follow through with the next Managed Services Cost Analysis appointment – don't lose momentum, it's difficult to gain back.

As soon as you return to your office, if you haven't already done so, modify the *Managed Services Thank-You Postcard** and *Managed Services Thank-You Email Template** with your

---

* *Included as a download*

company information and Logo, and get them to your Client immediately.

Wait a day or two, and then send your Client another *Managed Services Appointment Confirmation Postcard* and *Appointment Confirmation Email Template*, confirming your next meeting.

Tip:

It's important to maintain consistency in your Marketing process. Do not underestimate the value of the included Managed Services Postcards and Email Templates – when utilized properly, they will significantly improve your ability to close Managed Services Business.

The day before the appointment, call again and confirm. During this meeting, you will be utilizing the <u>*Managed Services Cost Analysis*</u>[*]. Simply follow the instructions included with this form to gather all of the required information you will need from your Client.

---

[*] *Included as a download*

DO NOT LEAVE THE COST ANALYSIS BEHIND FOR YOUR CLIENT TO FILL OUT!

Once this is complete, thank your Client for their time, and inform them that you will be compiling the results of your interview and preparing a Managed Services quote for them.

As soon as you return to your office, send your Client the *Managed Services Thank-You Postcard*[*] and *Thank-You Email*[*].

Wait a day or two, and then send your Client another *Managed Services Appointment Confirmation Postcard* and *Appointment Confirmation Email Template*, confirming your next meeting.

The day before the appointment, call and confirm. Present your Managed Services Cost Analysis findings with your Client, reiterate the benefits they will receive from your new model, address any concerns or objections they might have, and sign them up.

---

[*] *Included as a download*

We always bring along two copies of our Agreements, and countersign the signature page, after which we each keep a copy for our records.

Now when you return to your office, you're going to send a handwritten Thank-You Card, as well as sending your Client a *Special Thank You*. We use a local company that creates Cookie Bouquets. They have an incredible variety of different Cookies and unique designs for any occasion – and they deliver. Find a local vendor that provides a unique product that you can use as a *Special Thank-You* for your Clients – it will make a tremendous impression on them!

The final step is to modify the <u>*Managed Services Welcome Letter and Email Template*</u>* to include your Company information and Logo, if you haven't already done so, and send it to your Client.

The process for Marketing to new Clients is very similar, with the exception being the replacement of the Introduction Letter, Introduction Postcard and Introduction Email with the appropriate versions for New Clients on the download

---

* *Included as a download*

available after registering this book at
www.mspu.us/bookregistration. Follow the balance of the
process as indicated, with the utilization of the *New Client
Savings Analysis* for your data gathering.

Okay – let's summarize each step in our Managed Services
Marketing Process.

1. Send the initial Managed Services Marketing Letter
    and Email

2. Place a Phone Call to Set the Initial Appointment

3. Send the Managed Services Appointment Confirmation
    Postcard and Email

4. Conduct the First Client Meeting – Use the Managed
    Services Client PowerPoint Presentation

5. Send the Managed Services Thank-You Postcard and
    Email

6. Send the 2nd Managed Services Appointment
    Confirmation Postcard and Email

7. Conduct the Second Client Meeting – Use the Managed Services Cost or Savings Analysis

8. Send the 2nd Managed Services Thank-You Postcard and Email

9. Send the 3rd Managed Services Appointment Confirmation Postcard and Email

10. Conduct the Third Client Meeting – Present Findings and the Managed Services Agreement

11. Send a Handwritten Thank-You Card and Special Thank-You

12. Send Managed Services Welcome Letter and Email

Now this might seem like a lot of work, and that it takes a lot of time to execute – and we won't argue either of those points. You might even be thinking of cutting some corners and leaving out a step here or there, but for each step of this process that we have left out, over time our success rate has dropped accordingly. In fact, we have experienced situations where Clients have been so impressed with the quality of our materials and the consistency with which they were delivered, that they have rescheduled appointments just so that they could make sure all the "*Right*" people were available for us to present to.

Think about it this way - a Potential Client is basing their decision to hire you completely on your Materials, Message, Marketing Process and Presentation. They have no idea how really good (or really bad) you are before you begin providing Services to them.

It's like *Dating* someone new – if they're serious about entering into a committed relationship with you, they're watching your behavior whenever you're with them. And if you're equally serious, you're doing everything you can to impress them – picking them up, holding doors open for them, paying for dinner and entertainment (this goes both ways, ladies and gentlemen!), sending gifts, etc. This all happens *way* before the commitment, Wedding, whatever – as they have no real idea what things will actually be like in the future.

So I guess the analogy here is that your Materials, Message, Marketing Process and Presentation are how you Date your Client.

And how good a "Date" you are determines whether or not your Client will "Marry" you by signing your Managed Services Agreement!

Getting In The Door – The Importance of a Consistent Marketing Process

Eighty percent of success is showing up.

Woody Allen

No matter how beneficial our Managed Services Offerings may be to our Potential Clients, without a consistent Marketing process, we stand a poor chance of reaching them with our message.

If we want to be able to set increasing revenue goals and forecast future Earnings, we must develop, implement and maintain a Consistent Marketing Process.

Just as important as a Consistent Marketing Process is to your success, is the quality of the Marketing List you obtain - as it can make or break your Campaign. Generally, Marketing Lists with E-Mail Addresses are more expensive than those without.

Be certain you know who your Target Market is, as you can filter your Marketing Lists by the number of Desktops

in the environment, Employees, Geographic Location, Vertical Market Focus, Revenue, etc.

We have developed a formula that allows us the ability to set realistic Sales Goals through a simple mathematical exercise that you can also use to set your own Sales Goals, and Forecast future revenue.

The formula is very simple, and is comprised of several basic components:

- **Quality of Marketing List**
- **Number of Direct Mail Pieces Sent**
  - **Letters**
  - **Postcards**
- **Number of E-Mails Sent**
- **Number of Follow-Up Phone Calls Made**
- **Number of Appointments Set**
- **Number of Proposals Generated**
- **Number of Sales Closed**

So the success of the formula is directly related to how many of these activities are performed in a *consistent and timely manner*. If we do not perform these activities in the correct order, or skip some, or are inconsistent in their execution, then our results will suffer.

A well-developed Marketing Process, at a minimum, will include several different:

- **Direct Mail Letters**
- **Direct Mail Postcards**
- **E-Mail Templates**
- **Follow-Up Phone Calls**

Each one of these delivers one part of your message. We normally rotate the frequency of each of these types of Marketing Pieces, and mix in Testimonials from successful Business Wins (Win-Wires), normally in the form of E-Mail Templates. We've included a sample Win-Wire Template as a download available after registering this book at www.mspu.us/bookregistration for you to customize, and utilize in your Marketing efforts.

We then follow up on a series of Direct Mail and E-Mail Marketing Pieces with a series of Phone Calls. During these calls, we are verifying whether or not the Prospective Client has received our materials, and has any questions regarding our Services that we can answer for them.

If possible, we'll try to schedule an appointment for a FREE Network Evaluation during these calls. If we're unsuccessful, we keep these Prospective Clients on our E-Mail, Win-Wire and Newsletter list, and lessen the frequency with which we continue to contact them over time, but still continue to send them some form of messaging to them, at least monthly.

So our Marketing formula looks like this:

Number of Direct Mail Letters/Postcards/Emails Sent

+

Number of Follow-Up Phone Calls Made

=

Number of Appointments Set

=

Number of Proposals Generated

=

Number of New Managed Services Sales Closed

So, let's take an example where we want to increase our Managed Services revenue by $10,000 per month next quarter. And let's further assume that our average Managed

Services Agreement is worth $1,000. This means that we would need to sell about 10 new Clients an average Managed Services Agreement in order to meet our Sales Goal. How can our Marketing Formula help us?

In simple terms, we would need to determine what our Marketing Process would be. Let's say we decided to send 1 Introductory Letter, with a follow-up Postcard a week later to 1,000 Prospects. We then placed a Phone Call 3 days after the Postcards were mailed, and scheduled a couple of E-Mail Messages to be sent over the next several weeks. We would need to run this Marketing Campaign long enough to generate some meaningful statistics.

In this example, let's say we've run this particular Marketing Campaign for 90 days, and were able to set 15 appointments, which generated 11 Proposals, and we were able to close 6 New Clients. This is excellent! – I mean, we may have missed our Goal, but now we have statistics that we can use to modify our Marketing Process for the next Campaign!

Now we can try working with 2,000 Prospects, or throw in an additional Letter, or Postcard, to try to reach our Goal the next time around.

This process clearly illustrates how a Consistent Marketing Process can allow us the ability to Forecast future Earnings through a simple mathematical formula….

The important thing to remember is that whichever Process you develop for your Marketing Campaigns – remain consistent, and never stop sending some form of messaging to your Prospective Clients….

An Advanced Annuity-Based Revenue Philosophy

They always say time changes things, but you actually have to change them yourself.

Andy Warhol (1928 - 1987)

Now that we've had a pretty good overview of how to Market, Implement and Maintain a successful Managed Services model, let's explore extending the Annuity philosophy a bit, and see where it leads us.

We talked earlier about Exit Strategy, and came up with an example dealing with a target of about $83,000 per month in Annuity-Based Earnings to reach it, remember? We also came up with some numbers that showed how we could hit this goal by selling either $1,000 or $2,000 Managed Services Agreements. And lastly, we alluded to the option to sell our Clients additional Annuity-Based Services.

We'll explore this last topic here. If executed properly, this advanced concept could help you reach your hypothetical Earnings goal of $83,000 per month *much more quickly than selling Managed Services and Projects alone.* Here's how it works:

Let's take our organization as an example. We have identified our Core Deliverables (the Services we provide directly to our Clients) as:

1. LAN/WAN Infrastructure Design and Implementation

2. Managed Services

   a. Network Monitoring

   b. Remote Help Desk

   c. Vendor Management

3. Disaster Recovery Plans

Of these, all except the first service (Projects) afford us Annuity-based revenue. However; these are not the only services we deliver to our Clients.

We also provide the following additional Annuity-based services to our Clients through our *Fulfillment Partners:*

- VoIP

- Voice/PRI/LD

- T1/Integrated T1/Flex T1

- Hosting

- Web/Dev/DB

- Co-Location/DataCenter

- Cellular

- Remote Storage

- Phone Systems

- POS Processing

Our Fulfillment Partners are basically our Preferred Vendors – remember them? These are Vendors that deliver Services to our Clients, and pay us a commission for selling their Services, plus an Annuity each month thereafter. *In many cases the Annuity alone reaches tens of thousands of dollars per year, and on long multi-year Contracts can reach in the hundreds of thousands of dollars, depending on the Services or Solution.*

Add to this the fact that the Client normally pays us for our part in managing the design and implementation of these Services as well, and you can begin to appreciate the true scope of the additional Annuity-Based Revenue we can potentially receive.

This is a very powerful partnering concept that you should grasp and develop, if you haven't already. Executed properly, this concept can allow you to double, and even triple your revenue, without adding much additional Staff, other than a good Project Manager or two.

Of the Services that generated our organization's total revenue for FY2005, we fulfilled 60% of these directly, and our Fulfillment Partners fulfilled the remaining 40%.

With this philosophy, your objective is to manage the Client Relationship, and Project-Manage your Fulfillment Partners. Be advised – *this concept can succeed tremendously - or fail miserably*, based upon the quality of the Fulfillment Partners you choose, and how good you are at managing them.

We have learned extremely valuable lessons during the development of our Fulfillment Partnering concept. There are many pitfalls to avoid, but when executed properly, this advanced Partnering concept can change your business dramatically.

The tool we have developed that helps us determine which Services we should deliver to our Clients through Fulfillment Partners is the _Client Solution Roadmap_*. We discuss the proper utilization of this tool, along with all of the forms and tools included on the downloads available after registering this book at www.mspu.us/bookregistration in the following section.

---

* *Included as a download*

Appendix A

Managed Services Forms and Collateral Descriptions

We've included as a download available after registration at www.mspu.us/bookregistration each and every form, tool and piece of Marketing Collateral discussed in this book. These include:

- Managed Services Marketing Letter to Existing Clients

- Managed Services Marketing Email Template to Existing Clients

- Managed Services Marketing Letter to New Clients

- Managed Services Marketing Email Template to New Clients

- Managed Services Marketing Flyer

- Managed Services Appointment Confirmation Postcard Template

- Managed Services Appointment Confirmation Email Template

- Managed Services Thank-You Postcard Template

- Managed Services Thank-You Email Template

- Managed Services Profitability Matrix

- Managed Services Client Needs Analysis

- Managed Services Client Solution Roadmap

- Managed Services Existing Client Cost Analysis

- Managed Services New Client Savings Analysis

- Managed Services Vendor Management Form

- Managed Services Letter of Agency

- Managed Services Sample Agreement

- Managed Services Welcome Letter

- Managed Services Welcome Email Template

- Managed Services Win-Wire Email Template

- Managed Services Help Desk Escalation Process

- Managed Services Help Desk Graphical Call Routing Process

- Managed Services Client PowerPoint Presentation

- ***Bonus PowerPoint*** – Managed Services Legal Client Presentation

- ***Bonus PowerPoint*** – Managed Services Hosted VoIP Presentation

- ***Bonus PowerPoint*** – Managed Services Integrated T1 Presentation

- ***Extra Bonus*** – Microsoft TS2 Webcast hosted by Intelligent Enterprise: "The Secret to a Successful Managed Services Practice"

The following section describes each of these forms, tools and marketing materials in detail, and how to use them.

Managed Services Marketing Letter to Existing Clients – This letter is designed to "break the ice" with your existing Clients, and let them know that you are changing your business model to improve your support and response time to them. It also informs your Client that you will be calling them soon to discuss your transition.

Managed Services Marketing Email Template to Existing Clients – This professionally-prepared HTML Email Template can be branded with your company information, and reinforces the message in the Managed Services Marketing Letter to Existing Clients in a graphical manner.

Managed Services Marketing Letter to New Clients – This letter is geared towards New Client Acquisition, and does a great job of emphasizing the benefits of a Proactive IT Service. It also invites new Clients to receive a free Network and Security Health Checkup. We normally perform a Needs Analysis and run Microsoft Baseline Security Analyzer and provide a printout for the potential Client during this visit.

Managed Services Marketing Email Template to New Clients – A professionally-prepared HTML Email Template that can be branded with your company information, and reinforces the message in the Managed Services Marketing Letter to New Clients in a graphical manner.

Managed Services Marketing Flyer – A professionally-prepared Managed Services Color Flyer that can be branded with your company information.

Managed Services Appointment Confirmation Postcard Template – A professionally-prepared Postcard Template that can be branded with your company information and is used to confirm each and every Client Appointment.

Managed Services Appointment Confirmation Email Template – A professionally-prepared HTML Email Template that can be branded with your company information and is used to confirm each and every Client Appointment in a graphical manner.

Managed Services Thank-You Postcard Template – A professionally-prepared Postcard Template that can be branded with your company information and is used to thank your Clients after each appointment.

Managed Services Thank-You Email Template – A professionally-prepared HTML Email Template that can be branded with your company information and is used to thank your Clients after each appointment in a graphical manner.

Managed Services Profitability Matrix – A powerful tool that is used to document what you currently bill each and every one of your existing Clients on a yearly basis, and calculate what your Clients would be worth to you if they were transitioned to a Managed Services Model. It is used to insure that you never "under-bill" a Client for Managed Services.

Managed Services Needs Analysis – A comprehensive tool that is used to document a new Client's IT Pain Points, and is the basis for providing a Managed Services Value Proposition and Quote to address existing deficiencies.

Managed Services Client Solution Roadmap – A valuable tool that is used to document each and every Client's existing installed Solutions, as well as opportunities to sell them additional Annuity-Based Solutions.

Managed Services Existing Client Cost Analysis – An extremely effective tool used to *dollarize* your existing Client's lost revenue that can be recaptured through a Managed Services program.

Managed Services New Client Savings Analysis – An extremely effective tool used to *dollarize* a prospective Client's lost revenue that can be recaptured through a Managed Services program.

Managed Services Vendor Management Form – A comprehensive tool used to document each and every Vendor providing Services to your Client, including Contact and Account information. The information gathered with this form is used as the basis to create the Managed Services Letter of Agency.

Managed Services Letter of Agency – A powerful document that is used to establish your authority to manage Vendors on behalf of your Clients.

Managed Services Sample Agreement – A sample Managed Services Agreement included for instructional and informational purposes only, and is not recommended, or warranted for use. Always have your Attorney or Legal Team review any and all Agreements or Documents that you use in your IT Practice. Local laws and liabilities can never be fully covered by any type of generic document, including this Sample Managed Services Agreement.

Managed Services Welcome Letter – A letter welcoming your Client aboard, detailing their new Managed Services, and how they work. It also documents your Help Desk procedures, and how to open Trouble Tickets.

Managed Services Welcome Email Template – A professionally-prepared HTML Email Template that can be branded with your company information, and supports your Welcome Letter in a graphical manner.

Managed Services Win-Wire Email Template – A professionally-prepared HTML Email Template that can be branded with your company information, and allows you to market your recent Business Wins to Prospective Clients.

Managed Services Help Desk Escalation Process – A Basic Help Desk Escalation Process documenting Best Practices for Incident Handling.

Managed Services Help Desk Graphical Call Routing Process – A Visio Diagram graphically illustrating a Basic Help Desk Call Routing Process for Incident Handling.

Managed Services Client PowerPoint Presentation – An extremely effective Sales Presentation highlighting the benefits of a Managed Services program for the Client. This presentation can be run either as a Slideshow, or printed and placed in a Flip-Book for One-On-One Presentations.

- Bonus -

Managed Services Legal Vertical Client PowerPoint Presentation - An extremely effective and concise PowerPoint Presentation highlighting the benefits of a Managed Services Program for the Legal Client. This presentation can be run either as a Slideshow, or printed and placed in a Flip-Book for One-On-One Presentations.

- Bonus -

Managed Services Hosted VoIP Client PowerPoint Presentation - An extremely effective and concise PowerPoint Presentation highlighting the benefits of Hosted Voice over IP Services to the Client. This presentation can be run either as a Slideshow, or printed and placed in a Flip-Book for One-On-One Presentations.

- Bonus -

Managed Services Integrated T1 Client PowerPoint Presentation - An extremely effective and concise PowerPoint Presentation highlighting the benefits of an Integrated T1 to the Client. This presentation can be run either as a Slideshow, or printed and placed in a Flip-Book for One-On-One Presentations.

- Extra Bonus -

Microsoft TS2 Managed Services Presentation – A Managed Services Webcast conducted with the Microsoft TS2 Team, revealing our Core Methodologies, Deliverables and Sales Strategies. Includes Q&A from Attendees.

Managed Services Marketing Letter to Existing Clients

I'd like to take this opportunity to personally thank you for providing _____ the opportunity to earn your business through the years. I realize that we wouldn't be here without your support. I'd also like to take this opportunity to introduce you to some new cost-saving services we're rolling out in 200_.

As a result of our continuing effort to improve our services to you, we have developed a new and exciting Service Delivery Model. After many meetings with numerous Technology Vendors and much product testing, we are pleased to announce our new Flat-Rate IT and Managed Services offering.

These cutting-edge services are available to us now as a result of new technology developed over the last several years, which allows our Engineers and Support Staff to remotely manage and maintain your data network for one Flat Fee per month, saving you downtime and money.

In addition, our Managed Services offering allows us the ability to continually monitor your critical Network Servers, Devices and Line-of-Business Applications to insure maximum uptime 24 hours a day, 365 days a year. We've begun calling these new services "all you can eat", because during normal business hours, all of our remote support services are included in one flat, low monthly fee.

I'll be calling on you this month to discuss these new services with you, as well as your other IT needs. I'm certain that after our discussion, you'll see the benefit of these great new services, and how we can help you improve your IT Support infrastructure while reducing costs.

Thanks again for your continued support.

Sincerely,

Managed Services Marketing Email Template to Existing Clients

(Your Logo Here)

An Exciting Announcement..!

- (Your Company Name Here) is shifting to a Proactive Managed Services delivery model, which will allow us to support your entire Organization with our revolutionary Flat-Rate I.T. Program - *all for a fixed monthly cost!*
- Your Organization will benefit by receiving support beginning with our skilled Help-Desk Technicians all the way up to our Certified Network Engineers.
- You will
  - Save $$$ on Support Costs
  - Have one point of Contact for all of your Vendor-specific needs
  - Improve your I.T. Support Infrastructure
  - Elevate Employee Morale and Productivity
  - Benefit from Improved Uptime

Technology Consultants

(Your URL Here)

We'd like to personally thank you for providing (Your Company Name Here) the opportunity to earn your business through the years.

As a result of our continuing effort to improve our services to you, we have developed a new and exciting Service Delivery Model that will provide you with 24-Hour Systems Monitoring, Improved Response and Uptime, and save you downtime and money - *all for One Flat Fee Per Month!*

We will be calling you this month to discuss our valuable new services with you, as well as your other I.T. needs. We're certain that after our discussion, you'll see the benefit of these great new services, and how we can improve your I.T. Support while reducing costs.

Thanks again for your continued support!

(Your Logo/Certifications Here)

Flat-Rate I.T.

We support and maintain your entire Organization with our revolutionary Flat-Rate I.T. Program - *all for a fixed monthly cost.*

24x7x365 Network Monitoring

Our Network Monitoring Service never sleeps, and continuously monitors your network to insure maximum uptime. We take action as soon as a problem is detected.

Vendor Management

Quite possibly our most popular cost-saving Service. We manage all of your Vendor relationships, freeing you to focus on running your business. Whether it's an equipment, phone or network problem, we'll manage the issue to resolution.

(Your Company Name Here) takes pride in our ability to assist your Organization with all of your Information Technology and Telecommunications needs. Allow us the opportunity to custom-tailor our Consulting Services to your exact requirements.

(Your Contact Information Here)

Managed Services Marketing Letter to New Clients

Dear Fellow Business Owner,

Do you ever get frustrated when you need help with your computer systems, printers or Email? Does it ever seem that your systems only act up when you or your Staff need them the most? We take the confusion out of technology. Our goal is to give you a piece of mind.

The time has come!

We introduce Clients to new technologies that save them an average of 30% to 50% each year. We've proven that proactively managing your network always costs less than reacting to problems after they occur. We believe that your IT infrastructure should be a profit center for your business - not a cost center.

You deserve fast, affordable, professional support. That's why we've bundled our revolutionary Flat-Rate IT Support Program with our Proactive Network Monitoring Service, providing you experienced IT Support to maintain and protect your network 24 Hours a Day, 7 Days a Week, 365 Days a Year!

As an added bonus, if you call us right away, you'll be eligible to receive our most popular Service at no additional charge – Vendor Management, where we become the single point of contact for all or your Vendor issues. Free yourself to focus on running your business - not your Vendors.

Call us today…

If you are new to us, and would like to learn how to improve your IT Support while reducing costs, I'd like to invite you to a FREE Network and Security Health Checkup.

One of our Engineers will meet with you, discuss your concerns, and evaluate your network to insure you're getting the most out of the Technology you've already invested in. You'll know exactly where you stand from a Technology perspective after this **FREE** Service.

We offer this Service to you so that you can get to know us better without any risk, so please call us today!

Sincerely,

Managed Services Marketing Email Template to New Clients

(Your Logo Here)

Flat-Rate I.T. Support Is Here..!

- Imagine it - your entire Organization supported with our revolutionary Flat-Rate I.T. Program - *all for a fixed monthly cost*
- Your Organization will benefit by receiving support beginning with our skilled Help-Desk Technicians all the way up to our Certified Network Engineers.
- Save $$ on Support Costs
- One point of Contact
- Improve your I.T. Support Infrastructure
- Elevate Employee Morale and Productivity
- Monitored Systems = Improved Uptime

Technology Consultants

(Your URL Here)

Providing high quality, affordable Information Technology Consulting Services for Organizations of all sizes is our goal.

Need a first or second opinion before making a Technology-related business decision? Leverage our expertise, and allow us the opportunity to evaluate your current and future I.T. needs with you. In most cases, we can recommend effective, cost-saving strategies that improve productivity without breaking the bank.

Contact us at *(Your Number Here)*, and allow us the opportunity to provide you with a *Free Consultation* to discuss how your Organization could benefit from our Services.

(Your Logo/Certifications Here)

Flat-Rate I.T.

We support and maintain your entire Organization with our revolutionary Flat-Rate I.T. Program - *all for a fixed monthly cost*

24x7x365 Network Monitoring

Our Network Monitoring Service never sleeps, and continuously monitors your network to insure maximum uptime. We take action as soon as a problem is detected.

Vendor Management

Quite possibly our most popular cost-reducing Service. We manage all of your Vendor relationships, freeing you to focus on running your business. Whether it's an equipment, phone or network problem, we'll manage the issue to resolution.

[Your Company Name Here] takes pride in our ability to assist your Organization with all of your Information Technology and Telecommunications needs. Allow us the opportunity to custom-tailor our Consulting Services to your exact requirements.

[Your Contact Information Here]

Managed Services Marketing Flyer

(Your Logo Here)

Managed Services Appointment Confirmation Postcard Template

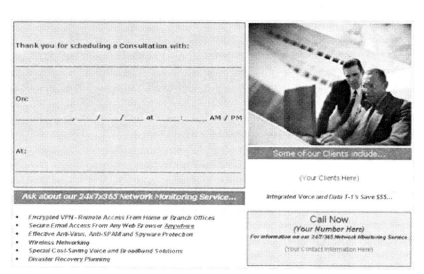

Managed Services Appointment Confirmation Email Template

(Your Logo Here)

Thank you for scheduling a Consultation

With:

On:

At:

Technology
Consultants

(Your URL Here)

Flat-Rate I.T.

Providing high quality, affordable Information Technology Consulting Services for Organizations of all sizes is our goal.

We support and maintain your entire Organization with our revolutionary Flat-Rate I.T. Program – *all for a fixed monthly cost*

Need a first or second opinion before making a Technology-related business decision? Leverage our expertise, and allow us the opportunity to evaluate your current and future I.T. needs with you. In most cases, we can recommend effective, cost-saving strategies that improve productivity without breaking the bank.

24x7x365 Network Monitoring

Contact us at *(Your Number Here)* and allow us the opportunity to provide you with a Free Consultation to discuss how your Organization could benefit from our Services.

Our Network Monitoring Service never sleeps, and continuously monitors your network to insure maximum uptime. We take action as soon as a problem is detected.

Vendor Management

(Your Logo/Certifications Here)

Quite possibly our most popular cost-saving Service. We manage all of your Vendor relationships, freeing you to focus on running your business. Whether its an equipment, phone or network problem, we'll manage the issue to resolution.

[Your Company Name Here] takes pride in our ability to assist your Organization with all of your Information Technology and Telecommunications needs. Allow us the opportunity to custom-tailor our Consulting Services to your exact requirements

[Your Contact Information Here]

Managed Services Thank-You Postcard Template

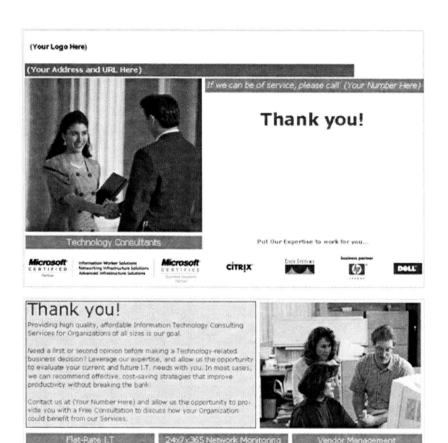

Managed Services Thank-You Email Template

(Your Logo Here)

Thank You!

- We sincerely appreciate the opportunity to earn your business.

- Our Technical Staff is ready to assist you with all of your Technology Needs.

- The courteous, professional manner in which we deliver our Services is the benchmark of our commitment to you.

Technology Consultants

(Your URL Here)

Flat-Rate I.T.

Providing high quality, affordable Information Technology Consulting Services for Organizations of all sizes is our goal.

Need a first or second opinion before making a Technology-related business decision? Leverage our expertise, and allow us the opportunity to evaluate your current and future I.T. needs with you. In most cases, we can recommend effective, cost-saving strategies that improve productivity without breaking the bank.

Contact us at (Your Number Here) and allow us the opportunity to provide you with a Free Consultation to discuss how your Organization could benefit from our Services.

We support and maintain your entire Organization with our revolutionary Flat-Rate I.T. Program – *all for a fixed monthly cost*.

24x7x365 Network Monitoring

Our Network Monitoring Service never sleeps, and continuously monitors your network to insure maximum uptime. We take action as soon as a problem is detected.

Vendor Management

Quite possibly our most popular consulting Service. We manage all of your Vendor relationships, freeing you to focus on running your business. Whether it's an equipment, phone or network problem, we'll manage the issue to resolution.

(Your Logo/Certifications Here)

(Your Company Name Here) takes pride in our ability to assist your Organization with all of your Information Technology and Telecommunications needs. Allow us the opportunity to custom-tailor our Consulting Services to your exact requirements.

(Your Contact Information Here)

Managed Services Profitability Matrix

This Excel Spreadsheet should be fairly self-explanatory. Simply enter in all of your existing Client's names in the far left column; along with the amount you billed them last year for SERVICE LABOR ONLY – no Project or Hardware billing. Then enter in the number of PC's, Network Printers, Networks and Servers you currently manage for them. The formulas in the spreadsheet will calculate what your yearly revenue would be if you transitioned them to a Managed Services program at $69 per PC, $29 per Network Printer, $99 per Network and $299 per Server per month.

Modify the Per PC formula until your Guaranteed Managed Services Revenue/Year matches your Existing Yearly Revenue as closely as possible. Use this tool to insure that you never quote an existing Client less for Managed Services than you have billed them in the past.

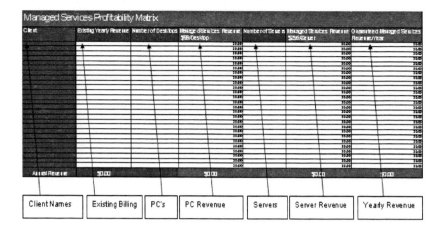

Managed Services Needs Analysis

Another self-explanatory 2-page form, the Needs Analysis is used to gather necessary data from a new Client's location in order to develop a Managed Services and/or additional Services Quote.

Needs Analysis

Section 1	Server		Proposal Date
	How Many Servers		
	Server OS	NT4 W2000 W2003 SBS	
	Number of Licenses		
	Size of Hard drives		
	Mirrored/Raid Hard drives	Yes or No	
	Server Manufacturer		
	Purchase Date		
	Server Proposal	Yes or No	

Section 2	Desktops	
	How Many Desktops	
	OS	W98 Win2k XP Pro Other
	How Many Remote Users	
	Spyware Problems	Yes or No
	Virus Problems	Yes or No
	Type of Anti-Virus Software	
	Type of Anti-Spyware Software	
	Internet Filtering	Yes or No
	Group Policy controls	Yes or No

Section 3	Back-Up Strategies	
	Back up Software	Veritas or Other
	Back Up Hardware	Internal or External
	Back Up Tapes (Type)	

Managed Services Client Solution Roadmap

The Client Solution Roadmap is a powerful tool used to document each and every Client's existing installed Hardware and Solutions, as well as opportunities to sell them additional Annuity-Based Solutions. List all of your Clients by name in the left column of the spreadsheet, and across the top of each row, identify every single Solution that your Clients need, even if you do not deliver those Solutions yourself.

Your task is to find additional Annuity-Based Fulfillment Partners to help you deliver all of these Solutions. If the Client's existing Hardware or Solution in each column does not meet your ideal for their environment, or is nonexistent, then they receive a RED Dot for that column. If they do, they receive a GREEN Dot for that column. This tool is 3'x4', so have it printed on a Plotter at your local Kinko's and hang it on a wall in your office – it needs to be large in order to display all of the data easily.

Your goal is to continue to sell and implement GREEN Dot
Solutions for each of your Clients. Keep track of the
percentage of GREEN Dots for each Client in the % Column.
This tool, when utilized properly, will insure that you are
regularly selling Solutions Deep into each and every one of
your Clients' environments. You may find that there are so
many opportunities to sell Solutions to your existing Clients by
utilizing this tool, that you may not need to market to new
Clients for a long, long time….

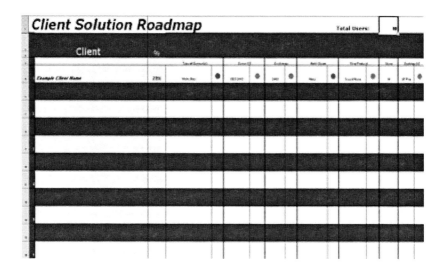

Managed Services Existing Client Cost Analysis

An extremely powerful tool, the Managed Services Existing Client Cost Analysis is used to graphically illustrate the benefits of a proactive Managed Services program to existing Clients, as it *dollarizes* revenue lost by the Client that is performing their own Vendor Management, as well as documenting their existing Reactive I.T. costs.

Simply fill in the blanks to come up with the Client's existing costs, determine what you will charge for Managed Services, and the formulas will do the rest. Use this as a Sales Tool to convince your Existing Clients to transition to Managed Services.

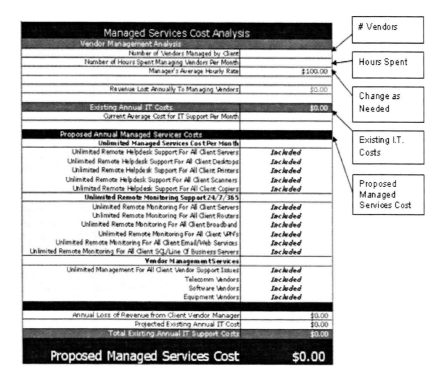

Managed Services Cost Analysis		
Vendor Management Analysis		
Number of Vendors Managed by Client		
Number of Hours Spent Managing Vendors Per Month		
Manager's Average Hourly Rate	$100.00	
Revenue Lost Annually To Managing Vendors	$0.00	
Existing Annual IT Costs	**$0.00**	
Current Average Cost for IT Support Per Month		
Proposed Annual Managed Services Costs		
Unlimited Managed Services Cost Per Month		
Unlimited Remote Helpdesk Support For All Client Servers	*Included*	
Unlimited Remote Helpdesk Support For All Client Desktops	*Included*	
Unlimited Remote Helpdesk Support For All Client Printers	*Included*	
Unlimited Remote Helpdesk Support For All Client Scanners	*Included*	
Unlimited Remote Helpdesk Support For All Client Copiers	*Included*	
Unlimited Remote Monitoring Support 24/7/365		
Unlimited Remote Monitoring For All Client Servers	*Included*	
Unlimited Remote Monitoring For All Client Routers	*Included*	
Unlimited Remote Monitoring For All Client Broadband	*Included*	
Unlimited Remote Monitoring For All Client VPN's	*Included*	
Unlimited Remote Monitoring For All Client Email/Web Services	*Included*	
Unlimited Remote Monitoring For All Client SQL/Line Of Business Servers	*Included*	
Vendor Management Services		
Unlimited Management For All Client Vendor Support Issues	*Included*	
Telecomm Vendors	*Included*	
Software Vendors	*Included*	
Equipment Vendors	*Included*	
Annual Loss of Revenue from Client Vendor Manager	$0.00	
Projected Existing Annual IT Cost	$0.00	
Total Existing Annual IT Support Costs	**$0.00**	

Proposed Managed Services Cost	**$0.00**

Callouts (right side):
- # Vendors
- Hours Spent
- Change as Needed
- Existing I.T. Costs
- Proposed Managed Services Cost

Managed Services New Client Savings Analysis

Very similar to the Managed Services Existing Client Cost Analysis, the Managed Services New Client Savings Analysis is used in the same fashion – but in a new Client's case, we can now additionally *dollarize* what Network Downtime is costing the Client, as well as the cost of their performing lightweight IT functions In-House, before calling their existing Reactive IT Service Provider. This successful tool allows us a tremendous amount of leverage in winning business.

Managed Services Savings Analysis - Example

Vendor Management Analysis

Number of Vendors Managed by Client	12
Number of Hours Spent Managing Vendors Per Month	10
Manager's Average Hourly Rate	$100.00
Revenue Lost Annually To Managing Vendors	$12,000.00

Revenue/Productivity Loss To Staff Performing IT Functions

Number of Hours Spent Performing IT Functions Per Month	10
Staff Member's Average Hourly Rate	$100.00
Revenue Lost Annually To Performing IT Functions	$12,000.00

Revenue Loss To Network Downtime

Number of Users On Client Network	20
Number of Servers At Client Location	3

Network Downtime	Hours
Email Services Down per Month	4
Internet Connection Down per Month	4
Server or Desktops Down per Month	2
Total Hours Network is Down Monthly	10
Total Hours Network is Down Annually	120

Labor Costs	
Average Salary Per Employee	$30,000.00
Total Employee Yearly Payroll	$600,000.00
Average Annual Employee Hours	2080
Total Annual Employee Hours	41600
Average Hourly Labor Cost Per Employee	$14.42
Revenue Lost To Downtime Annually	$34,615.38

Existing Annual IT Costs

	$7,800.00
Current Average Cost for IT Support Per Month	$650.00

Proposed Managed Services Costs

	$18,000.00
Unlimited Managed Services Cost Per Month	$1,500.00
Unlimited Remote Helpdesk Support For All Client Servers	Included
Unlimited Remote Helpdesk Support For All Client Desktops	Included
Unlimited Remote Helpdesk Support For All Client Printers	Included
Unlimited Remote Helpdesk Support For All Client Scanners	Included
Unlimited Remote Helpdesk Support For All Client Copiers	Included
Unlimited Remote Monitoring Support 24/7/365	
Unlimited Remote Monitoring For All Client Servers	Included
Unlimited Remote Monitoring For All Client Routers	Included
Unlimited Remote Monitoring For All Client Broadband	Included
Unlimited Remote Monitoring For All Client VPN's	Included
Unlimited Remote Monitoring For All Client Email/Web Services	Included
Unlimited Remote Monitoring For All Client SQL/Line Of Business Servers	Included
Vendor Management Services	
Unlimited Management For All Client Vendor Support Issues	Included
Telecomm Vendors	Included
Software Vendors	Included
Equipment Vendors	Included

Annual Loss of Revenue from Client Vendor Management	$12,000.00
Annual Loss of Revenue from Staff Performing IT Functions	$12,000.00
Annual Loss of Labor Cost from Network Downtime	$34,615.38
Projected Existing Annual IT Cost	$7,800.00

Total Existing Annual IT Support Costs

	$66,415.38
Projected Managed Services Cost	$36,000.00

Total Client Savings $30,415.38

Losses

Managed Services Vendor Management Form

Self-explanatory and the basis for the data used to prepare the Managed Services Letter of Agency, this document contains all of the necessary Contact and Service Account information for all of the Client's Vendors.

Vendor Management

Database Vendor

Account Number	
Last Date of Service	
Address/City/State/Zip	
Contract Terms	
Contact Person/Account Rep	
Account Rep Phone number	
Account Rep Email Address	
Average Monthly Bill	
Performance Status 1-5	

Website/Email Vendor

Account Number	
Last Date of Service	
Address/City/State/Zip	
Contract Terms	
Contact Person/Account Rep	
Account Rep Phone number	
Account Rep Email Address	
Average Monthly Bill	
Performance Status 1-5	

IT Vendor

Account Number	
Last Date of Service	
Address/City/State/Zip	
Contract Terms	
Contact Person/Account Rep	
Account Rep Phone number	
Account Rep Email Address	
Average Monthly Bill	
Performance Status 1-5	

Printer/Stationery Vendor

Account Number	
Last Date of Service	
Address/City/State/Zip	
Contract Terms	
Contact Person/Account Rep	
Account Rep Phone number	
Account Rep Email Address	
Average Monthly Bill	
Performance Status 1-5	

Phone Service Vendor

Account Number	
Last Date of Service	
Address/City/State/Zip	

Managed Services Letter of Agency

A critical form used for Vendor Management. The appropriate information is completed on this form for each of the Client's Vendors, and then printed on the Client's Letterhead. After the Client signs each Letter of Agency, they are mailed to each Vendor. A follow-up call is then made to each Vendor to confirm that they have received the Letter of Agency and overcome any concerns or objections each Vendor may have.

SAMPLE LETTER OF AGENCY

Have the following letter copied on to your Client's company letterhead:

DATE

Vendor Contact Name

Vendor Name

Vendor Address

Vendor City, State, Zip

Re: (CLIENT ACCOUNT NUMBER WITH VENDOR)

To Whom It May Concern:

We the undersigned, hereby authorize (YOUR COMPANY NAME) to act on our behalf in all manners relating to our Services and Agreements with (VENDOR NAME), including negotiating, authorizing, scheduling or canceling Services, and signing of all documents relating to these matters. Any and all acts carried out by (YOUR COMPANY NAME) on our behalf shall have the same effect as acts of our own.

This authorization is valid until further written notice from (CLIENT COMPANY NAME).

Sincerely,

(Client Company counsel or Client Company Officer Signature)

(Name and Title)

Managed Services Welcome Letter

A letter welcoming your Client aboard, and detailing their new Services, and how they work. It also documents your Help Desk Procedures, and how to open Trouble Tickets.

Sample Welcome Letter

Congratulations and Welcome to (Your Company Name) – your Premier Managed IT Solution Provider.

Since (Inception Date), (Your Company Name) has been developing and implementing Information Technology Solutions that improve our Clients' Business Processes, adding value to their Bottom Line.

Our new Managed Services Plan is a direct result of our continual effort to identify our Clients' needs, and alleviate their business pain.

We are pleased and excited to introduce this valuable Service to you and your Organization. We are now your IT Department, and will provide Technical Support for each User and Device on your Network, as detailed in your Managed Services Agreement.

Your Managed Services Plan provides you with Unlimited Help Desk/Remote Support during the hours of 8am and 5pm Monday through Friday, excluding Holidays. Should your Support need fall outside of these hours; you will be billed as indicated in Appendix "B" of your Managed Services Agreement.

In addition to providing you with Unlimited Help Desk/Remote Support, we will also monitor your Servers and their Critical Services such as Exchange, SQL Databases, and other specific Line-Of-Business Applications installed on them, along with your Internet Connection and Firewall/Routers 24 hours a day, 7 days a week.

Should any of these Services fail, our Network Monitoring Systems will attempt to restart them. Should these attempts fail, a Trouble Ticket will be created immediately, and an Engineer will be alerted to begin troubleshooting. Our goal is to minimize your downtime, and this is just one tool that we rely on to achieve this objective.

We've made it simple to request Support – just send an Email to:

(Your Helpdesk Email Address)

Or, just ask for the Help Desk at (Your Helpdesk Phone Number).

If calling after hours with an Emergency, please dial extension (Your After-Hours Extension), and an On-Call Engineer will be paged immediately.

Vendor Management is also included in your Managed Services Plan. We relieve you of the burden of having to manage all of your Vendors, and allow you the ability to focus on running your business.

You will be contacted shortly by a Customer Service Representative who will gather the information we will need in order to begin providing this valuable Service to you, and to schedule a visit from our Technical Team so that we can begin configuring your Network for Managed Services.

Thank you again for allowing us the opportunity to earn your business. In a short time, I'm sure you'll agree that we're adding tremendous value to your Organization through our Managed Services.

Sincerely,

Managed Services Welcome Email Template

(Your Logo Here)

Welcome to Managed Services..!

- We are pleased and excited to welcome you and your Organization to Managed Services. We are now your I.T. Department, and will provide Technical Support for each User and Device on your Network, as detailed in your Managed Services Agreement.

- We've made it simple to request Support – just send an Email to: (Your Helpdesk Email Address)

- Or, just ask for the Help Desk at (Your Helpdesk Phone Number). *If calling after hours with an Emergency, please dial extension (Your After-Hours Extension), and an On-Call Engineer will be paged immediately.*

Technology Consultants

(Your URL Here)

Your Managed Services Plan provides you with *Unlimited Help Desk/Remote Support* during the hours of 8am and 5pm Monday through Friday, excluding Holidays.

In addition to providing you with Unlimited Help Desk/Remote Support, we will also monitor your Servers and their Critical Services such as Exchange, SQL Databases, and other specific Line-Of-Business Applications installed on them, along with your Internet Connection and Firewall/Routers 24 hours a day, 7 days a week.

Our goal is to minimize your down time, and this is just one tool that we rely on to achieve this objective.

Vendor Management is also included in your Managed Services Plan. We relieve you of the burden of having to manage all of your Vendors, and allow you the ability to focus on running your business.

You will be contacted shortly by a Customer Service Representative who will gather the information we will need in order to begin providing this valuable Service to you, and to schedule a visit from our Technical Team so that we can begin configuring your Network for Managed Services.

Thank you again for allowing us the opportunity to earn your business. In a short time, I'm sure you'll agree that you're adding tremendous value to your Organization through our Managed Services.

Flat-Rate I.T.

We support and maintain your entire Organization with our revolutionary Flat-Rate I.T. Program – *all for a fixed monthly cost*

24x7x365 Network Monitoring

Our Network Monitoring Service never sleeps, and continuously monitors your network to ensure maximum uptime. We take actions soon as a problem is detected.

Vendor Management

Quite possibly our most popular cost-saving Service. We manage all of your Vendor relationships, freeing you to focus on running your business. Whether it's an equipment, phone or network problem, we'll manage the issue to resolution.

(Your Logo/Certifications Here)

(Your Company Name Here) takes pride in our ability to assist your Organization with all of your Information Technology and Telecommunications needs. Allow us the opportunity to custom-tailor our Consulting Services to your exact requirements.

[Your Contact Information Here]

Managed Services Win-Wire Email Template

(Your Logo Here)

(One Line Subject about your solution here)

Background

(Describe existing environment and Pain Points before your arrival.)

Solution

Technology
Consultants

(Describe your Solution, and how it addressed the Client's Pain.)

(Your URL Here)

(Your Contact Information Here)

Managed Services Help Desk Escalation Process

1. Support Request is Received
2. Trouble Ticket is Created
3. Issue is Identified and documented in Help Desk system
4. Issue is qualified to determine if it can be resolved through Tier 1 Support

If issue can be resolved through Tier 1 Support:

5. Level 1 Resolution - issue is worked to successful resolution
6. Quality Control –Issue is verified to be resolved to Client's satisfaction
7. Trouble Ticket is closed, after complete problem resolution details have been updated in Help Desk system

If issue cannot be resolved through Tier 1 Support:

6. Issue is escalated to Tier 2 Support
7. Issue is qualified to determine if it can be resolved by Tier 2 Support

If issue can be resolved through Tier 2 Support:

8. Level 2 Resolution - issue is worked to successful resolution

9. Quality Control –Issue is verified to be resolved to Client's satisfaction
10. Trouble Ticket is closed, after complete problem resolution details have been updated in Help Desk system

If issue cannot be resolved through Tier 2 Support:

9. Issue is escalated to Tier 3 Support
10. Issue is qualified to determine if it can be resolved through Tier 3 Support

If issue can be resolved through Tier 3 Support:

11. Level 3 Resolution - issue is worked to successful resolution
12. Quality Control –Issue is verified to be resolved to Client's satisfaction
13. Trouble Ticket is closed, after complete problem resolution details have been updated in Help Desk system

If issue cannot be resolved through Tier 3 Support:

12. Issue is escalated to Onsite Support
13. Issue is qualified to determine if it can be resolved through Onsite Support

If issue can be resolved through Onsite Support:

14. Onsite Resolution - issue is worked to successful resolution

15. Quality Control –Issue is verified to be resolved to Client's satisfaction
16. Trouble Ticket is closed, after complete problem resolution details have been updated in Help Desk system

If issue cannot be resolved through Onsite Support:

17. I.T. Manager Decision Point – request is updated with complete details of all activity performed

Managed Services Help Desk Graphical Service Call Routing Process

HELP DESK SERVICE CALL ROUTING PROCESS

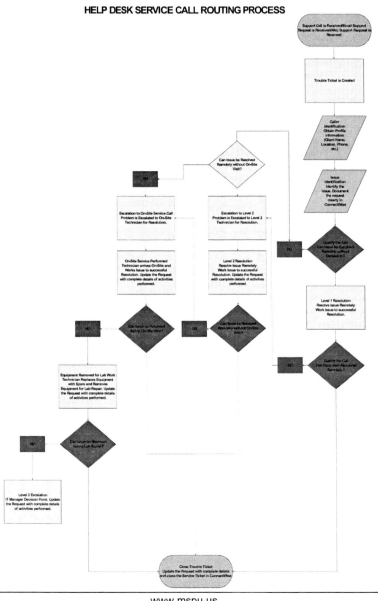

Managed Services Sample Agreement

This Sample Managed Service Agreement is included for instructional and informational purposes only, and is not recommended, nor warranted for use.

Always have legal counsel review any and all Agreements or Documents that you utilize in your IT Practice, or distribute to your Clients prior to doing so.

Local laws and liabilities can never be fully covered by any type of generic document, including this Sample Managed Service Agreement.

Managed Services Sample Agreement

1.   Term of Agreement

This Agreement between

_____, herein referred to

as Client, and _____,

hereinafter referred to as Service Provider, is effective

upon the date signed, and shall remain in force for a

period of three years. The Service Agreement

automatically renews for a subsequent three year term

beginning on the day immediately following the end of

the Initial Term unless either party gives the other

ninety days' prior written notice of its intent not to

renew this Agreement.

  a) This Agreement may be terminated by either Party
      upon ninety (90) days' written notice if the other
      Party:

      a. Fails to fulfill in any material respect its
          obligations under this Agreement and
          does not cure such failure within thirty (30)
          days' of receipt of such written notice.

      b. Breaches any material term or condition

of this Agreement and fails to remedy such breach within thirty (30) days' of receipt of such written notice.

    c.   Terminates or suspends its business operations, unless it is succeeded by a permitted assignee under this Agreement.

  b) If either party terminates this Agreement, Service Provider will assist Client in the orderly termination of services, including timely transfer of the services to another designated provider. Client agrees to pay Service Provider the actual costs of rendering such assistance.

2.   Fees and Payment Schedule

Fees will be $_____ per month, invoiced to Client on a Monthly basis, and will become due and payable on the first day of each month. Services will be suspended if payment is not received within 5 days following date due. Refer to Appendix B for services covered by the monthly fee under the terms of this Agreement.

It is understood that any and all Services requested by Client that fall outside of the terms of this Agreement will be considered Projects, and will be quoted and billed as separate, individual Services.

3.   **Taxes**

It is understood that any Federal, State or Local Taxes applicable shall be added to each invoice for services or materials rendered under this Agreement. Client shall pay any such taxes unless a valid exemption certificate is furnished to Service Provider for the state of use.

4.   **Coverage**

Remote Helpdesk and Vendor Management of Client's IT networks will be provided to the Client by Service Provider through remote means between the hours of 8:00 am – 5:00 pm Monday through Friday, excluding public holidays. Network Monitoring Services will be provided 24/7/365. All services qualifying under these conditions, as well as Services that fall outside this scope will fall under the provisions of Appendix B.

Hardware costs of any kind are not covered under the terms of this Agreement.

Support and Escalation

Service Provider will respond to Client's Trouble Tickets under the provisions of Appendix A, and with best effort after hours or on holidays. Trouble Tickets must be opened by Client's designated I.T. Contact Person, by email to our Help Desk, or by phone if email is unavailable. Each call will be assigned a Trouble Ticket number for tracking. Our escalation process is detailed in Appendix A.

Service outside Normal Working Hours

Emergency services performed outside of the hours of 8:00 am – 5:00 pm Monday through Friday, excluding public holidays, shall be subject to provisions of Appendix B.

Service Calls Where No Trouble is found

If Client requests onsite service and no problem is found or reproduced, Client shall be billed at the current applicable rates as indicated in Appendix B.

Limitation of Liability

In no event shall Service Provider be held liable for indirect, special, incidental or consequential damages arising out of service provided hereunder, including but not limited to loss of profits or revenue, loss of use of equipment, lost data, costs of substitute equipment, or other costs.

5.   Additional Maintenance Services

Hardware/System Support

Service Provider shall provide support of all hardware and systems specified in Appendix B, provided that all Hardware is covered under a currently active Vendor Support Contract; or replaceable parts be readily available, and all Software be Genuine, Currently Licensed and Vendor-Supported. Should any hardware or systems fail to meet these provisions, they will be excluded from this Service Agreement. Should 3rd Party Vendor Support Charges be required in order to resolve any issues, these will be passed on to the Client after first receiving the Client's authorization to incur them.

Virus Recovery for Current, Licensed Antivirus protected systems

Damages caused by, and recovery from, virus infection not detected and quarantined by the latest Antivirus definitions are covered under the terms of this Agreement. This Service is limited to those systems protected with a Currently Licensed, Vendor-Supported Antivirus Solution.

Monitoring Services

Service Provider will provide ongoing monitoring and security services of all critical devices as indicated in Appendix B. Service Provider will provide monthly reports as well as document critical alerts, scans and event resolutions to Client. Should a problem be discovered during monitoring, Service Provider shall make every attempt to rectify the condition in a timely manner through remote means.

6. Suitability of Existing Environment

Minimum Standards Required for Services

In order for Client's existing environment to qualify for
Service Provider's Managed Services, the following
requirements must be met:

1. All Servers with Microsoft Windows Operating
   Systems must be running Windows 2000
   Server or later, and have all of the latest
   Microsoft Service Packs and Critical Updates
   installed.
2. All Desktop PC's and Notebooks/Laptops with
   Microsoft Windows Operating Systems must be
   running Windows XP Pro or later, and have all
   of the latest Microsoft Service Packs and
   Critical Updates installed.
3. All Server and Desktop Software must be
   Genuine, Licensed and Vendor-Supported.
4. The environment must have a currently
   licensed, up-to-date and Vendor-Supported
   Server-based Antivirus Solution protecting all
   Servers, Desktops, Notebooks/Laptops, and
   Email.

5. The environment must have a currently licensed, Vendor-Supported Server-based Backup Solution.
6. The environment must have a currently licensed, Vendor-Supported Hardware Firewall between the Internal Network and the Internet.
7. Any Wireless data traffic in the environment must be secured with a minimum of 128bit data encryption.

Costs required to bring Client's environment up to these Minimum Standards are not included in this Agreement.

7.   Excluded Services

Service rendered under this Agreement does not include:

1)   Parts, equipment or software not covered by vendor/manufacturer warranty or support.
2)   The cost of any parts, equipment, or shipping charges of any kind.

3) The cost of any Software, Licensing, or Software Renewal or Upgrade Fees of any kind.

4) The cost of any 3rd Party Vendor or Manufacturer Support or Incident Fees of any kind.

5) The cost to bring Client's environment up to minimum standards required for Services.

6) Failure due to acts of God, building modifications, power failures or other adverse environmental conditions or factors.

7) Service and repair made necessary by the alteration or modification of equipment other than that authorized by Service Provider, including alterations, software installations or modifications of equipment made by Client's employees or anyone other than Service Provider.

8) Maintenance of Applications software packages, whether acquired from Service Provider or any other source unless as specified in Appendix B.

9) Programming (modification of software code) and program (software) maintenance unless as specified in Appendix B.

10)   Training Services of any kind.

8.   Miscellaneous

This Agreement shall be governed by the laws of the State of _____. It constitutes the entire Agreement between Client and Service Provider for monitoring/maintenance/service of all equipment listed in "Appendix B." Its terms and conditions shall prevail should there be any variance with the terms and conditions of any order submitted by Client.

Service Provider is not responsible for failure to render services due to circumstances beyond its control including, but not limited to, acts of God.

9.   Acceptance of Service Agreement

This Service Agreement covers only those services and equipment listed in "Appendix B." Service Provider must deem any equipment/services Client may want to add to this Agreement after the effective date acceptable. The addition of equipment/services not listed in "Appendix B" at the signing of this Agreement, if acceptable to Service Provider, shall result in an adjustment to the Client's monthly charges.

IN WITNESS WHEREOF, the parties hereto have caused this Service Agreement to be signed by their duly authorized representatives as of the date set forth below.

Accepted by:

_____

Authorized Signature   Service Provider   Date

_____

Authorized Signature   Client   Date

Managed Services Agreement
Appendix A

Response and Resolution Times

The following table shows the targets of response and resolution times for each priority level:

Trouble	Priority	Response time (in hours) *	Resolution time (in hours) *	Escalation threshold (in hours)
Service not available (all users and functions unavailable).	1	Within 1 hour	ASAP – Best Effort	2 hours
Significant degradation of service (large number of users or business critical functions affected)	2	Within 4 hours	ASAP – Best Effort	4 hours
Limited degradation of service (limited number of users or functions affected, business process can continue).	3	Within 24 hours	ASAP – Best Effort	48 hours
Small service degradation (business process can continue, one user affected).	4	within 48 hours	ASAP – Best Effort	96 hours

Support Tiers

The following details and describes our Support Tier levels:

Support Tier	Description
Tier 1 Support	All support incidents begin in Tier 1, where the initial trouble ticket is created, the issue is identified and clearly documented, and basic hardware/software troubleshooting is initiated.
Tier 2 Support	All support incidents that cannot be resolved with Tier 1 Support are escalated to Tier 2, where more complex support on hardware/software issues can be provided by more experienced Engineers.
Tier 3 Support	Support Incidents that cannot be resolved by Tier 2 Support are escalated to Tier 3, where support is provided by the most qualified and experienced Engineers who have the ability to collaborate with 3rd Party (Vendor) Support Engineers to resolve the most complex issues.

Managed Services Agreement
Appendix A (cont)
Service Request Escalation Procedure

1. Support Request is Received
2. Trouble Ticket is Created
3. Issue is Identified and documented in Help Desk system
4. Issue is qualified to determine if it can be resolved through Tier 1 Support

If issue can be resolved through Tier 1 Support:

5. Level 1 Resolution - issue is worked to successful resolution
6. Quality Control –Issue is verified to be resolved to Client's satisfaction
7. Trouble Ticket is closed, after complete problem resolution details have been updated in Help Desk system

If issue cannot be resolved through Tier 1 Support:

6. Issue is escalated to Tier 2 Support
7. Issue is qualified to determine if it can be resolved by Tier 2 Support

If issue can be resolved through Tier 2 Support:

8. Level 2 Resolution - issue is worked to successful resolution
9. Quality Control –Issue is verified to be resolved to Client's satisfaction
10. Trouble Ticket is closed, after complete problem resolution details have been updated in Help Desk system

If issue cannot be resolved through Tier 2 Support:

9. Issue is escalated to Tier 3 Support
10. Issue is qualified to determine if it can be resolved through Tier 3 Support

If issue can be resolved through Tier 3 Support:

11. Level 3 Resolution - issue is worked to successful resolution
12. Quality Control –Issue is verified to be resolved to Client's satisfaction
13. Trouble Ticket is closed, after complete problem resolution details have been updated in Help Desk system

If issue cannot be resolved through Tier 3 Support:

12. Issue is escalated to Onsite Support
13. Issue is qualified to determine if it can be resolved through Onsite Support

If issue can be resolved through Onsite Support:

14. Onsite Resolution - issue is worked to successful resolution

15. Quality Control –Issue is verified to be resolved to Client's satisfaction

16. Trouble Ticket is closed, after complete problem resolution details have been updated in Help Desk system

If issue cannot be resolved through Onsite Support:

17. I.T. Manager Decision Point – request is updated with complete details of all activity performed

Managed Services Agreement

Appendix A (cont)

HELP DESK SERVICE CALL ROUTING PROCESS

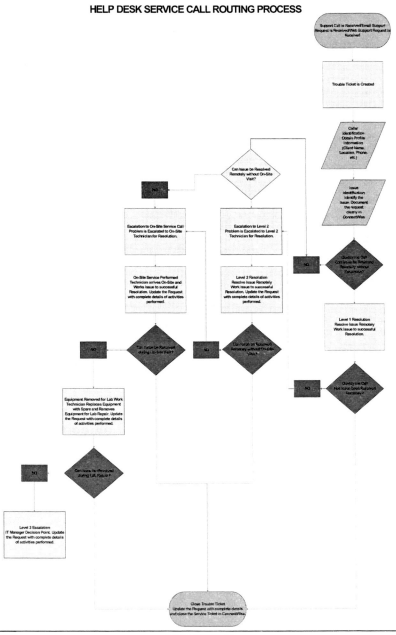

Managed Services Agreement
Appendix B

Description	Frequency	Included in Maintenance
General		
Document software and hardware changes	As performed	YES
Test backups with restores	Monthly	YES
Monthly reports of work accomplished, work in progress, etc.	Monthly	YES
Systems		
Check print queues	As needed	YES
Ensure that all server services are running	Daily/hourly	YES
Keep Service Packs, Patches and Hotfixes current as per company policy	Monthly	YES
Check event log of every server and identify any potential issues	As things appear	YES
Monitor hard drive free space on server, clients	Daily/hourly	YES
Reboot servers if needed	As needed	YES
Run defrag and chkdsk on all drives	As needed	YES
Scheduled off time server maintenance	As needed	YES
Install software upgrades	As needed	YES
Determine logical directory structure, Implement, MAP, and detail	Revisit Monthly	YES
Set up and maintain groups (accounting, admin, printers, sales, warehouse, etc)	As needed	YES
Check status of backup and restores	Daily	YES
Alert office manager to dangerous conditions -Memory running low -Hard drive showing sign of failure -Hard drive running out of disk space -Controllers losing interrupts -Network Cards report unusual collision activity	As needed	YES
Educate and correct user errors (deleted files, corrupted files, etc.)	As needed	YES
Clean and prune directory structure, keep efficient and active	Monthly	YES
Disaster Recovery		
Disaster Recovery of Server(s)	As Needed	YES

Managed Services Agreement
Appendix B (cont.)

Networks

Check router logs	Weekly	YES
Performance Monitoring/Capacity Planning	Weekly	YES
Monitor DSU/TSU, switches, hubs and internet connectivity, and make sure everything is operational (available for SNMP manageable devices only)	Weekly	YES
Major SW/HW upgrades to network backbone, including routers, WAN additions, etc.	As needed	YES
Maintain office connectivity to the Internet	Ongoing	YES

Security

Check firewall logs	Monthly	YES
Confirm that antivirus virus definition auto updates have occurred	As Needed	YES
Confirm that virus updates have occurred	As Needed	YES
Confirm that backup has been performed on a daily basis	Daily	YES
Create new directories, shares and security groups, new accounts, disable/delete old accounts, manage account policies	As Needed	YES
Permissions and file system management	As Needed	YES
Set up new users including login restrictions, passwords, security, applications	As needed	YES
Set up and change security for users and applications	As needed	YES
Monitor for unusual activity among users	Ongoing	YES

Apps

Exchange user/mailbox management	As needed	YES
Monitor directory replication	As needed	YES
Monitor WINS replication	As needed	YES
SQL server management	As needed	YES
Overall application disk space management	As needed	YES
Ensure Microsoft Office Applications are functioning as designed	As needed	YES

Managed Services Agreement
Appendix B (cont)

Service Rates

Labor	Rate
Remote PC Management/Help Desk 8am-5pm M-F	INCLUDED
Remote Printer Management 8am-5pm M-F	INCLUDED
Remote Network Management 8am-5pm M-F	INCLUDED
Remote Server Management 8am-5pm M-F	INCLUDED
24x7x365 Network Monitoring	INCLUDED
Lab Labor 8am-5pm M-F	INCLUDED
Onsite Labor 8am-5pm M-F	INCLUDED
Remote PC Management/Help Desk 5:01pm-9pm M-F	$_____/hr
Remote Printer Management 5:01pm-9pm M-F	$_____/hr
Remote Network Management 5:01pm-9pm M-F	$_____/hr
Remote Server Management 5:01pm-9pm M-F	$_____/hr
Lab Labor 5:01pm-9pm M-F	$_____/hr
Onsite Labor 5:01pm-9pm M-F	$_____/hr
Remote Labor All Other Times	$_____/hr
Lab Labor All Other Times	$_____/hr
Onsite Labor All Other Times	$_____/hr

Covered Equipment

Managed Desktops: Desktops/Notebooks
Managed Printers:
Managed Networks:
Managed Servers:

Appendix B

Managed Services Client PowerPoint Presentation

5 Easy Ways to Save $$$ With Technology
-or-
How to Immediately Improve Your Bottom Line

---

1. Flat-Rate I.T. Services

- Support and maintain your entire Organization Remotely
- Phone Support
- Remote Assistance (Desktop Sharing)
- Live Meeting (Online Collaboration)
- State-Of-The-Art Trouble-Ticketing System
- Automated Escalation Process
- Onsite Support As Needed

All for One Fixed Monthly Cost!

2. Managed Services

- 24x7x365 Network Monitoring
- Over 255 Events/Services Monitored
- Critical Services Automatically Restarted
- Immediate Alerting
- Automated Trouble-Ticket Generation
- Automated Escalation Process
- Proactive *not Reactive*

Insures Maximum Uptime for Critical Equipment

www.managedservicesuniversity.com   Copyright 2006 Intelligent Enterprise, Inc.   3

3. Vendor Management

- *Our Most Popular $$$-Saving Service*
- Manage all Vendor Relationships
  - Phone and Internet Service and Providers
- All Voice or Data Network-Connected Equipment
  - Phone Systems
  - Faxes
  - Scanners
  - Copiers
- Proprietary Software Applications

Frees You to Focus on Running Your Business –
Not Your Vendors

www.managedservicesuniversity.com   Copyright 2006 Intelligent Enterprise, Inc.   4

4. Professional Services

* Technology Solution Design and Development
* Proof-of-Concept Lab Testing
* Onsite Implementation
* Project Management
* Disaster Recovery Planning and Response
* Intrusion Detection and Security Testing
* Secure Point-to-Point VPN Design
* Co-Location Services for High-Availability Services

We Create a Technology Plan that Serves Your Mission

www.managedservicesuniversity.com   Copyright 2006 Intelligent Enterprise, Inc.   5

---

5. Software and Application Development

* Custom Database Design and Maintenance
* Custom Application Development
* Web-Enabling Application Services
* Legacy Application Rewrites
* Custom Report Generation
* Hosting Services for High Availability

Existing Data Migration to New Applications

www.managedservicesuniversity.com   Copyright 2006 Intelligent Enterprise, Inc.   6

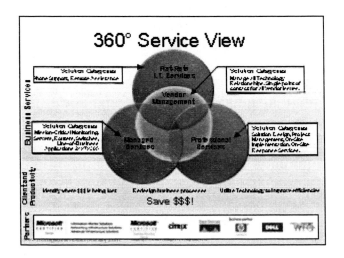

Cost-Saving Services

* Flat-Rate I.T. Services
  * *Immediate I.T. Savings*
* Managed Services
  * *Proactive Monitoring for Long-Term Savings*
* Vendor Management
  * *Immediate Impact to the Bottom Line*
* Professional Services
  * *We get it right the First Time, Every Time*
* Software and Application Development
  * *Eliminate Redundant Data Entry and Improve Efficiency*

You Can't Afford Not to Start Saving $$$ With Us!

www.managedservicesuniversity.com   Copyright 2006 Intelligent Enterprise, Inc.   8

Appendix C

Managed Services Legal Client PowerPoint Presentation

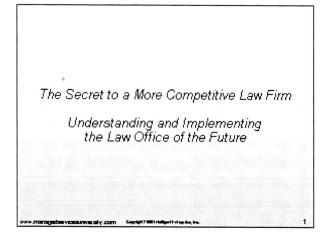

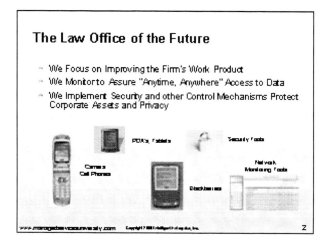

Technology Challenges Facing Law Firms

* Mobility
  * Remote access to Email, Document Management Systems, Billing and Time Keeping Systems
* Availability
  * Printer and Resource Uptime Reliability
* Disaster Recovery
  * Disaster Recovery Planning, Testing and Implementation
* Security
  * Securing confidential client records Internally and Externally
* Help Desk and Network Support
  * Limited Access to Technical Resources

www.managedservicesunweekly.com   Copyright 2008 Intelligent Enterprise, Inc.   3

We Can Help

* Insure Availability of Data and Case Management Resources – databases and client records
* Maintain 24x7x365 Monitoring and Security for Maximum Uptime
* Significantly Reduce IT Costs and Complexity
* Assure Attorneys and Remote Users have Mobile Access to Email and Data

www.managedservicesunweekly.com   Copyright 2008 Intelligent Enterprise, Inc.   4

Flat-Rate I.T. Services

- Support and maintain your entire Organization Remotely
- Phone Support
- Remote Assistance (Desktop Sharing)
- Live Meeting (Online Collaboration)
- State-Of-The-Art Trouble-Ticketing System
- Automated Escalation Process
- Onsite Support As Needed

All for One Fixed Monthly Cost!

Managed Services

- 24x7x365 Network Monitoring
- Over 255 Events/Services Monitored
- Critical Services Automatically Restarted
- Immediate Alerting
- Automated Trouble-Ticket Generation
- Automated Escalation Process
- Proactive *not Reactive*

Insures Maximum Uptime for Critical Equipment

Vendor Management

* *Our Most Popular $$$-Saving Service*
* Manage all Vendor Relationships
    * Phone and Internet Service and Providers
* All Voice or Data Network-Connected Equipment
    * Phone Systems
    * Faxes
    * Scanners
    * Copiers
* Proprietary Software Applications

Frees You to Focus on Running Your Business – Not Your Vendors

www.managedservicesuniversity.com   Copyright 2006 Intelligent Enterprise, Inc.   7

Professional Services

* Technology Solution Design and Development
* Proof-of-Concept Lab Testing
* Onsite Implementation
* Project Management
* Disaster Recovery Planning and Response
* Intrusion Detection and Security Testing
* Secure Point-to-Point VPN Design
* Co-Location Services for High-Availability Services

We Create a Technology Plan that Serves Your Mission

www.managedservicesuniversity.com   Copyright 2006 Intelligent Enterprise, Inc.   8

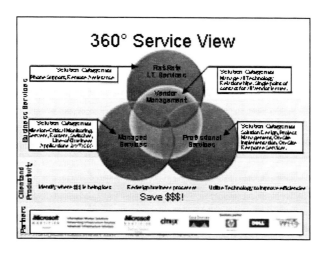

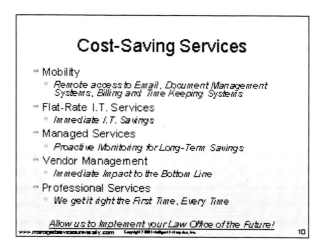

Appendix D

Managed Services Hosted VoIP PowerPoint Presentation[*]

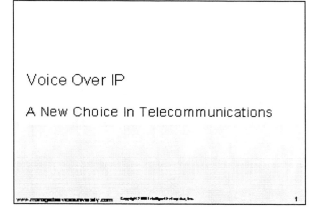

---

[*] *Slide Deck Courtesy of I-Tel – www.itel-ip.com*

Now there's a Better Way!

Hosted Voice Over IP Service
for Business

www.managedservicesuniversity.com   Copyright © Intelligent Enterprise, Inc.   3

Why Hosted VoIP Service?

- No more headaches
- Inexpensive to implement
- Simple to control, configure, customize
- No more upgrades (i.e., protection from obsolescence)
- Unparalleled productivity gains
- Scale according to your needs

www.managedservicesuniversity.com   Copyright © Intelligent Enterprise, Inc.   4

Why Hosted VoIP Service?

- PBX or Centrex replacement services uoted Product of the Year 2003 by *Internet Telephony Magazine*

- Hosted IP uoice seruice for local and long distance uoice
  - Indiuidual handset phone number assignment and dial-tone
  - Long list of Class 5 features
  - Intra-enterprise priuate dial plan management

- Hosted IP uoice seruices prouide
  - IP-enabled productiuity tools for managing moues, adds, changes
  - Web- and audio-based conferencing seruice
  - One box for fax, uoice, uoicemail, and e-mail (unified messaging)
  - Web-based portal for end-user management and personalization

www.managedseruicesuniuersity.com   Copyright 2005 Intelligent Enterprise, Inc.   5

How will VoIP
make your life simpler?

www.managedseruicesuniuersity.com   Copyright 2005 Intelligent Enterprise, Inc.   6

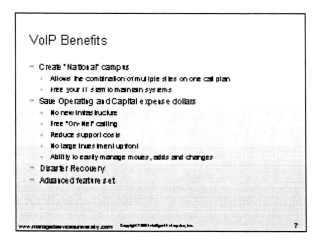

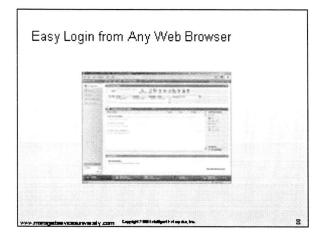

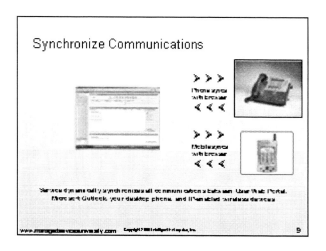

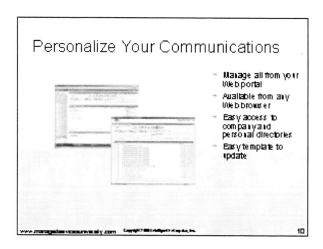

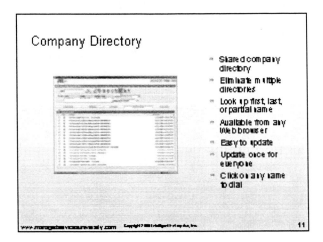

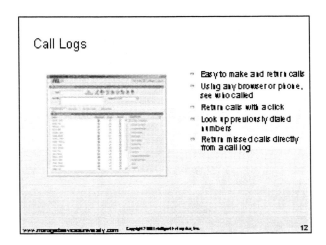

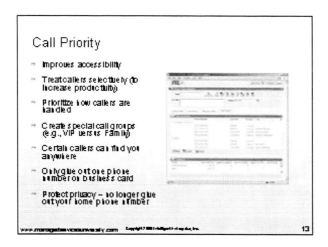

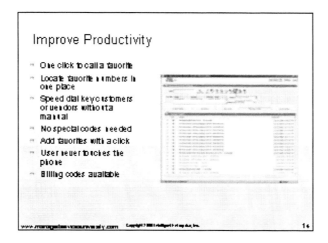

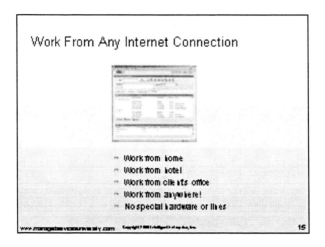

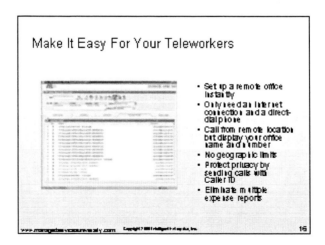

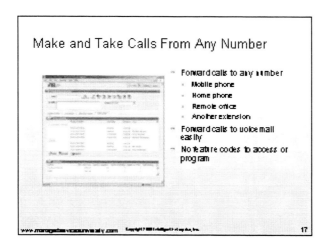

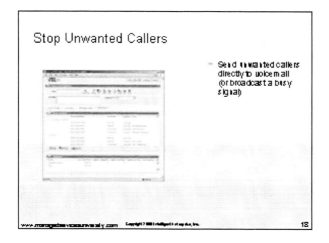

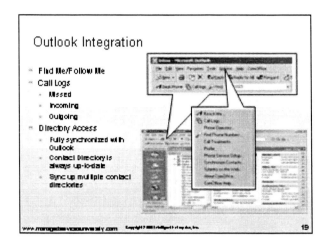

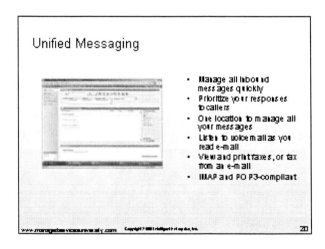

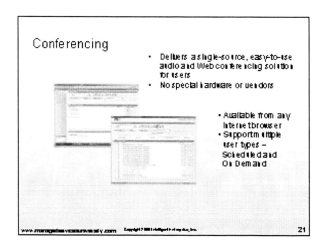

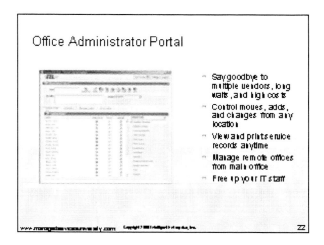

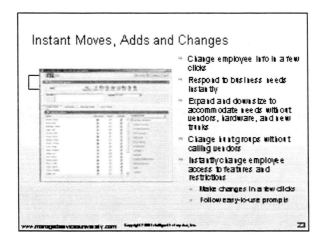

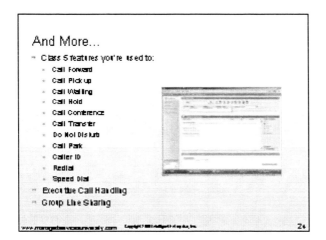

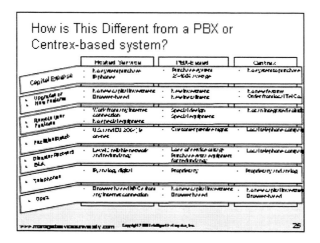

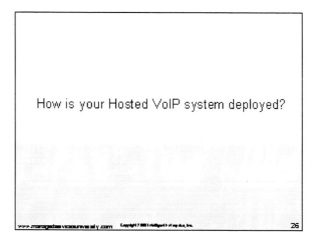

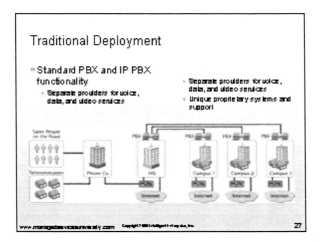

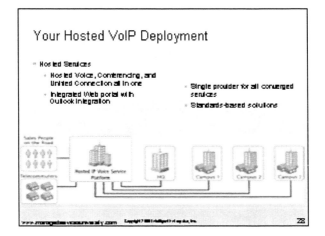

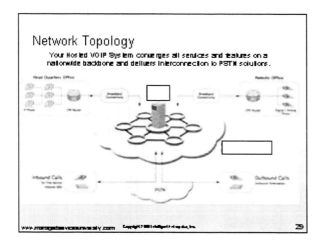

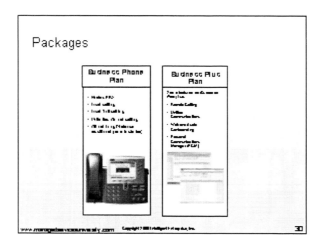

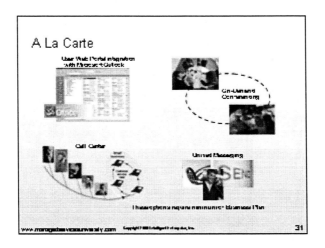

Access Options

* T-1
* NxT1
* DS3
* DSL
* Any existing Broadband
  Connection*

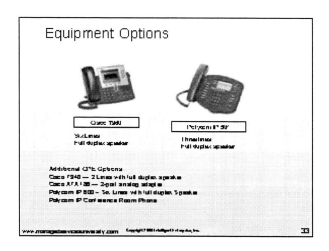

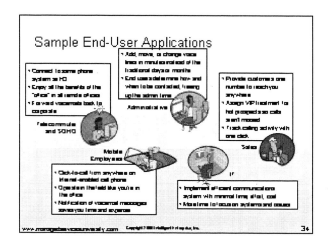

Are You a Candidate for Hosted VoIP?

* Is the phone a critical part of your business?
* Is your business highly collaborative? Do you use conferencing today?
* Want to eliminate the costs and management associated with branch offices?
* Do you have a mobile sales force?
* Is your business focused on customer service?
* Do you anticipate rapid or uncertain growth?
* Are you planning an office move soon?
* Are you looking for increases in business productivity?
* Do you want control and management over moves, adds, and changes?
* Do you want to eliminate costly upgrades or expansion?
* Do you want immediate access to new features?

www.managedservicesuniversity.com   Copyright 2008 Intelligent Enterprise, Inc.   35

As We End Our Session

* Increases your productivity
* Cuts monthly telecom costs
* Scales with your needs
* Simple to control, configure, and customize
* Allows you to focus on your business instead of your communications systems

www.managedservicesuniversity.com   Copyright 2008 Intelligent Enterprise, Inc.   36

Appendix E

Managed Services Integrated T1 PowerPoint Presentation

Integrated T1's for Voice and Data

A New Choice In Telecommunications

Combined Voice and Data Circuits

- More economical than separate Voice and Broadband Services
- Extremely Customizable
- Network Management and Monitoring 24/7/365
- Simple, Competitive Pricing
- Bundle all of your Local, Long Distance and High-Speed Internet
- Start with as few as 4 Voice Lines and 1024 Kbps of Broadband
- Easy to add Voice Lines – scale according to your needs
- Email Services and Web Hosting Packages Available
- Simple, Integrated Invoice
- Inexpensive to Implement

How does your current service stack up?

Integrated T1 Voice Features

- Line Hunting
- 3-Way Calling
- Six-Way Calling
- Speed Call 8
- Call Transfer
- Call Hold
- Variable Call Forwarding
- Remote Call Forwarding
- Call Pickup Group
- Directed Call Pickup
- Call Park

How does your current service stack up?

www.managedservicesuniversity.com   Copyright 2008 Intelligent Enterprise, Inc.   3

Integrated T1 Data Features

- Provides a Dedicated Digital Channel for access to the Internet
- Speeds range from 265K to 1.544M
- Router Included
- Up to 128 Email Addresses Included
- Domain Name Hosting Included

How does your current service stack up?

www.managedservicesuniversity.com   Copyright 2008 Intelligent Enterprise, Inc.   4

Are You a Candidate for an Integrated T1?

* Is the phone a critical part of your business?

* Want to reduce the costs and management associated separate Voice and Data Services?

* Do you anticipate rapid or uncertain growth?

* Are you planning an office move soon?

* Are you looking for increases in business productivity?

www.managedservicesuniversity.com   Copyright ? Intelligent Enterprise, Inc.   5

As We End Our Session

* Increases your productivity

* Cuts monthly telecom costs

* Scales with your needs

* Simple to control, configure, and customize

* Simplified Invoicing allows you to focus on your business

www.managedservicesuniversity.com   Copyright ? Intelligent Enterprise, Inc.   6

Index

What's On The Download?

- Managed Services Marketing Letter to Existing Clients
- Managed Services Marketing Email Template to Existing Clients
- Managed Services Marketing Letter to New Clients
- Managed Services Marketing Email Template to New Clients
- Managed Services Marketing Flyer
- Managed Services Appointment Confirmation Postcard Template
- Managed Services Appointment Confirmation Email Template
- Managed Services Thank-You Postcard Template
- Managed Services Thank-You Email Template
- Managed Services Profitability Matrix
- Managed Services Client Needs Analysis
- Managed Services Client Solution Roadmap
- Managed Services Client Cost Analysis
- Managed Services Client Savings Analysis
- Managed Services Vendor Management Form
- Managed Services Letter of Agency

- Managed Services Sample Agreement
- Managed Services Welcome Letter
- Managed Services Welcome Email Template
- Managed Services Win-Wire Email Template
- Managed Services Help Desk Escalation Process
- Managed Services Help Desk Graphical Service Call Routing Process
- Managed Services Client PowerPoint Presentation
- *Bonus PowerPoint* – Managed Services Legal Client Presentation
- *Bonus PowerPoint* – Managed Services Hosted VoIP Presentation
- *Bonus PowerPoint* – Managed Services Integrated T1 Presentation
- *Extra Bonus* – Microsoft TS2 Webcast on Managed Services Hosted By Intelligent Enterprise

To receive the downloadable forms, tools and collateral discussed in this book, as well as exclusive additional sales and marketing resources and valuable webinar training absolutely FREE, register your copy of The Guide to a Successful Managed Services Practice at www.mspu.us/bookregistration today!

MSP University

MSP University specializes in providing managed services training, workshops, and boot camps, as well as sales and marketing services to IT service providers, vendors and channel organizations worldwide through our online Managed Services Provider University at www.mspu.us.

With hundreds of Webinars, TeleSeminars, forms, tools and collateral, MSP University is the single, most comprehensive vendor agnostic resource that SMB IT Service Providers can utilize to help build, operate and grow a successful I.T. solutions and managed services practice.

When we began researching and developing our Managed Services business model years ago, there did not exist a single resource that we could reference in order to increase our knowledge in this vast area. This made it an extremely difficult and time-consuming process to engage all of the Vendors, test all of the Tools, develop all of the Business and Technical Processes and create the Sales and Marketing Techniques necessary to transition to a successful Managed Services Provider.

Our hundreds of best-practices focused Courses Cover topics such as:

- Managed Services Concepts
- MSP Vendor Management
- MSP HR Training
- MSP Marketing Process
- MSP Lead Generation
- MSP Sales Process
- MSP Appointment Setting
- MSP Sales Closing Techniques
- MSP Help Desk Best Practices
- MSP Tools
- MSP Service Contracts
- MSP Staffing
- MSP Vendor Solution Partnering
- MSP Additional Annuity-Based Solutions

And more…this is an extremely small sampling of our Courses…

In addition, Regional Live Workshops, Boot Camps and One-On-One Managed Services Consulting Services are included for our Managed Services University Attendees.

The Guide To A Successful Managed Services Practice

To join MSP University absolutely FREE and to find out how we can help you become more successful as a Managed Services Provider, visit us at:

www.mspu.us/join

You can also subscribe to our Newsletter here:

www.mspu.us/news

And our blog here:

www.mspu.us/blog

Make certain to register this book to access and download all of the forms, tools and collateral covered within, and receive regular updates other special offers at:

www.mspu.us/bookregistration

Also check out all of our other Managed Services books and companion audiobooks available at www.mspu.us, including "The Best I.T. Sales & Marketing BOOK EVER!" and "The Best I.T. Service Delivery BOOK EVER!"